T0323919

# Cambridge Elements ≡

### Elements in the Problems of God
edited by
Michael L. Peterson
*Asbury Theological Seminary*

# THE TRINITY

## Scott M. Williams
*University of North Carolina, Asheville*

Shaftesbury Road, Cambridge CB2 8EA, United Kingdom

One Liberty Plaza, 20th Floor, New York, NY 10006, USA

477 Williamstown Road, Port Melbourne, VIC 3207, Australia

314–321, 3rd Floor, Plot 3, Splendor Forum, Jasola District Centre,
New Delhi – 110025, India

103 Penang Road, #05–06/07, Visioncrest Commercial, Singapore 238467

Cambridge University Press is part of Cambridge University Press & Assessment,
a department of the University of Cambridge.

We share the University's mission to contribute to society through the pursuit of
education, learning and research at the highest international levels of excellence.

www.cambridge.org
Information on this title: www.cambridge.org/9781009565189

DOI: 10.1017/9781009293105

When citing this work, please include a reference to the DOI 10.1017/9781009293105

First published 2024

*A catalogue record for this publication is available from the British Library*

ISBN 978-1-009-56518-9 Hardback
ISBN 978-1-009-29311-2 Paperback
ISSN 2754-8724 (online)
ISSN 2754-8716 (print)

# The Trinity

Elements in the Problems of God

DOI: 10.1017/9781009293105
First published online: December 2024

Scott M. Williams
*University of North Carolina, Asheville*

**Author for correspondence:** Scott M. Williams, swillia8@unca.edu

**Abstract:** The doctrine of the Trinity, proclaimed by Christians through the Nicene-Constantinople creed, is foundational to traditional Christian belief and worship of God. But is this doctrine logically coherent? How can there be three divine persons (Father, Son, and Holy Spirit), each is God, and yet there is only one God? This is a fundamental question for philosophers, but theologians have additional questions. This Element addresses philosophical and theological issues concerning the Trinity: hermeneutical and logical problems, personal pronouns, monarchy, equality, the *filioque* debate, real relations, unity of action, self-knowledge in the Trinity, and simplicity. Based on the author's recent rediscovery of the sixth ecumenical council's (Constantinople III) clarifications of Trinitarian doctrine, this Element introduces Conciliar Trinitarianism and shows how it responds to the issues, including a resolution to the fundamental logical question. It also compares Conciliar Trinitarianism with Miaphysite, neo-Sabellian, Social, and other models of the Trinity.

**Keywords:** Trinity, Conciliar Trinitarianism, theism, logical problem of the Trinity, self-knowledge in the Trinity

ISBNs: 9781009565189 (HB), 9781009293112 (PB), 9781009293105 (OC)
ISSNs: 2754-8724 (online), 2754-8716 (print)

# Contents

# 1 The Trinity: An Introduction

## 1.1 Setting the Stage: Conciliar Trinitarianism

Jews, Christians, and Muslims are monotheists. They proclaim that there is one and only one God. They worship God, who is said to be the only one worthy of our highest worship and praise. God is all-knowing, all-powerful, and all-good. God is the creator of everything that exists that is not God. In addition to all this, most Christians believe that there are three hypostases (persons) who are God: God the Father, God the Son, and God the Holy Spirit. Christians who do not believe that there are three hypostases, each of whom is God, call themselves Christian Unitarians (Tuggy 2021a). This Element focuses on the traditional Christian belief that the Father, Son, and Holy Spirit are each God. This Christian belief is traditional in the sense that it is an ancient belief expressed in different ways in the New Testament (e.g., through different literary conventions; see Hill 2015; Smith 2023), it was the subject of careful reflection by Christians, and there were ecumenical councils that made proclamations about what to believe, and what not to believe, with regard to the Trinity. Even more, Trinitarian beliefs were a feature of ancient Christian worship such that prayers in the liturgy reflected this belief about the Trinity. What motivated these beliefs about the Father, Son, and Holy Spirit has to do with the incarnation, death, and resurrection of Jesus Christ and the revelation of the Holy Spirit in the life of Jesus and at Pentecost (John 1:1–18; Acts of the Apostles 2:1–43; see Athanasius 2011: 87–127). It is through their understanding of divine revelation that Christians came to believe that the Father, Son, and Holy Spirit are each the one God. For example, Jesus taught his disciples to baptize new believers "in the name of the Father, the Son, and the Holy Spirit" (Matthew 28:19). It is beyond the scope of this Element to engage in reporting in detail Christian interpretations of the Old Testament and the New Testament with regard to the Trinity. Nevertheless, Section 3.2 discusses a key question about the relation between the Father and "the one God." This issue bears directly on how to interpret various passages from the Bible that associate the Father and the one God.

Let it suffice to say that for traditional Christians, it was the conjunction of those historical events plus careful interpretation of these Scriptures that motivated later Christians to offer clarifications or theories of the Trinity to dispel confusion, misunderstanding, or the appearance of logical contradiction. A fundamental philosophical challenge to Trinitarian theology is the conjunction of apparently inconsistent claims: There is one and only one God, and there are three different persons and yet each of them is the one God. This is the logical problem for the Trinity, and it is what most philosophers of religion have focused on in discussing the Trinity. I discuss this logical problem in Section 2.3.

Other challenges to a coherent account of the Trinity derive from this problem, but not all. For example, what does it mean for an entity to be a "person"? The term "person" meant something different in the ancient and medieval discussions than what it came to mean after early modern European philosophy (Van Dyke 2019; Williams 2020b). Some contemporary philosophical theologians assume some sort of modern account of personhood and then use that to articulate their model of the Trinity or use their modern concept of a person to interpret ancient or medieval philosophical theologians when they write about divine persons (see Section 1.6). This has led to a quagmire between more historically minded philosophical theologians today and those either less familiar with the original languages or the history and who insist on what seems intuitive regarding divine personhood or personhood in general.

Christian churches have proclaimed the Trinity based on divine revelation or interpretation of divine revelation, or church teaching, and not based on a priori reasoning. So, if one is going to engage philosophically with "the Trinity," then one must engage with the history of Christian discussion and teaching to understand key terms of art and the criteria for evaluating a model of the Trinity. Unfortunately, if one is neutral regarding other theological matters such as theological authority or a trusted guiding source, then it is not straightforward in how to come to an agreement on criteria for evaluating a model of the Trinity. This is another problem for Trinitarian theology, which is independent of the logical problem. It is the problem of shared criteria for evaluating models of the Trinity: Whose criteria? (See McCall 2010.)

Philosophical theologians with different prior beliefs or theological commitments may have different criteria, or even ways of identifying relevant criteria, for evaluating a model of the Trinity. This suggests that debates about the Trinity are like other debates in philosophy: The same argument might be persuasive to one philosopher/theologian but unpersuasive to another philosopher/theologian. This disagreement may be because there are other background conditions (e.g., other beliefs, commitments, or experiences) that shape how the argument is received. Even if both philosophers/theologians were to accurately report those relevant background conditions to each other, they still might have different judgments about the persuasiveness of the argument. If they exchange information about the different background conditions, then that *might* change how confident (or how justified) each is in their assessment of the original argument. But, if a philosophical theologian is committed to a particular Christian tradition (e.g., Eastern Orthodox, Roman Catholic, Anglican, Lutheran, Presbyterian, Oriental Orthodox, Baptist, etc.) and learns that their tradition has supported, or ruled out, a given understanding of the Trinity, then that might persuade them to revise their preferred model or confidence in that model.

It is outside the scope of this Element to narrate the many different ecclesial beliefs or commitments. Since it is traditional Christian belief regarding the Trinity that is often the target of objections, this Element focuses on what the first seven ecumenical councils have to say about the Trinity. I choose the first seven because most Christians, historically speaking, are a part of a church that accepts these ecumenical councils as infallible guides to theology or as authoritative but fallible guides to theology. It is one thing to appeal to a favored theologian for statements and insights about the Trinity, and quite another to appeal to what an ecumenical council has taught about the Trinity. Given the theological authority (however conceived) and liturgical significance of these ecumenical councils, any serious contemporary reflection on the Trinity ought to engage with them.

I use the term "Conciliar Trinitarianism" to refer to what these ecumenical councils say about the Trinity. By focusing on these councils, we will be able to see how Conciliar Trinitarianism fares regarding various (apparent) problems. I will, however, discuss models of the Trinity that are inconsistent with Conciliar Trinitarianism. Some of these alternative models are popular in contemporary literature, and so it will be useful to grasp why they are inconsistent with Conciliar Trinitarianism, and what objections they face.

Lastly, this Element engages with history, philosophy, and theology. Each of these disciplines is needed for serious discussion of the Trinity. Readers trained in philosophy may find the history challenging (or prima facie irrelevant), but perseverance will be rewarded with a more complex understanding of what is philosophically interesting and inspiring in contemplating the Trinity. Readers trained in history or theology may find the philosophy challenging (or prima facie irrelevant), but attention to philosophical details (e.g., different logical relations) will be rewarded with better understandings of lesser-known theological areas of investigation (see Sections 3–5).

## 1.2 A Brief History

Origen of Alexandria introduced two terms into the context of theorizing about the Trinity, namely "hypostasis" and "ousia" (see Kelly 1968: 128–132). (Another term that was used was "prosopon"; in many cases theologians used "hypostasis" and "prosopon" as synonyms or co-extensive in their reference.)[1] However, Origen did not give much clarification about how we ought to understand his use of these terms. What was clear was that "hypostasis" was predicated of each of them: God the Father is a hypostasis, God the Son is

---

[1] This history is selective; for greater historical coverage, see Kelly 1968; Grillmeier 1975, 1986, 1995, 1996, 2013; Ayres 2004; Anatoloios 2011.

a different hypostasis, and God the Holy Spirit is a yet another hypostasis. The Greek term "ousia" ("being") is the abstract noun of the verb "to be." "Ousia" could mean different things (Stead 1977). Whatever the precise meaning that Origen had in mind, it at least was used to refer to the Father's divine nature, which is shared with the Son and Holy Spirit. Origen suggested that God the Father eternally emanates God the Son and God the Holy Spirit. In some sense, the Son and the Holy Spirit derive from the Father. In one text, Origen admits that the Son is "another God" (Origen of Alexandria 1992: 58–60). Arius of Alexandria (and later Aetius and Eunomius) argued that only the Father is God, and that the Son and Holy Spirit are each a different hypostasis compared to each other and to the Father, *and* that each has their own "ousia" that is different in kind to the Father's "ousia." This understanding presents the Son and Holy Spirit as lesser Gods compared to the Father. But Athanasius of Alexandria argued against this interpretation of Origen and of the Bible, and against Arius's understanding of God's revelation in Jesus Christ and the Holy Spirit. For Athanasius, the Father shares their very own "ousia" and "hypostasis" with the Son and the Holy Spirit (see Prestige 1969: 167; Paasch 2010). Athanasius did not work out a general theory to distinguish "ousia" and "hypostasis," but he clearly argued that the Son and the Holy Spirit are each the same God as the Father because they share the Father's "ousia," and so they are not lesser, or other, Gods than the Father.

In AD 325 at the Council of Nicaea, Christian bishops and priests composed a proclamation of faith, which was called the Nicene creed, or the Symbol of the Faith (see Tanner 1990: 1–19). This was regarded as the first ecumenical council. A key passage in this creed was the sentence that says that Jesus Christ is "God from God, light from light, true God from true God, begotten not made, consubstantial [*homoousion*] with the Father [. . .]" (Tanner 1990: 5). The inclusion of "homoousion" was key in rejecting what Arius had claimed about the Father and the Son. At the end of this creed, Arius's claims were explicitly rejected, particularly his claim that "there was a time when the Son was not." The Nicene creed proclaims that the Father and Son are eternally the Father and the Son *and* they are the same with regard to "ousia." The first divine hypostasis does not become a Father through a temporal generation of the Son; rather, the Father is always the Father, the Son is always the Son.

The Nicene creed proclaims the Holy Spirit ("We believe in the Holy Spirit"), but it does not say much about the Holy Spirit. But in AD 381, the second ecumenical council, which took place in Constantinople, made some clarifications with regard to the Holy Spirit. It says that the Holy Spirit is "the Lord and giver of Life, who proceeds from the Father, and is co-worshiped and co-glorified with the Father and Son [. . .]" (Tanner 1990: 24). The clarification distinguishes how the Son and the Holy Spirit each relate to the Father. The Son is "begotten" from the Father, and the Holy Spirit "proceeds" from the Father. Between the first and the second ecumenical councils, theologians engaged in exegesis of the New Testament to find clarification on how the Son and the Holy Spirit are each from the Father (see Gregory of Nyssa 1954: 38–39; Gregory of Nazianzus 2002: 120–125; Basil the Great 2011). A key passage was found in the *Gospel According to John* 15:26, which says that the Holy Spirit is the one "who proceeds from the Father" (Revised Standard Version). By the thirteenth century, the Roman Catholic church added to the Nicene creed that the Holy Spirit "proceeds from the Father *and the Son* (*filioque*)" (Tanner 1990: 230, 526–527). This was, and remains, a source of significant disagreement between the Eastern Orthodox and the Roman Catholic churches. The dispute about the *filioque* not only is historically significant as a source of division between ancient Christian churches, but it also raises interesting philosophical issues regarding the nature and exercise of powers (see Section 3.4). While it seems to be a common practice in contemporary philosophical theology to set aside the issue of the *filioque*, nevertheless it is a core issue in Trinitarian theology. So, I discuss it and argue for a (new) position that mediates between the two sides, while leaning more toward the Eastern Orthodox side.

Eunomius, like Arius, raised questions about the ontological status of the Father, Son, and Holy Spirit (see Batilo 2018). He claimed that God is not caused to exist. Creatures exist only because they are caused to exist, but God is not caused to exist. If the Father eternally causes the Son, as Christians were teaching, then the Son is not God. Likewise, if the Father eternally causes the Holy Spirit, then the Holy Spirit is not God. Consequently, the Father's being and nature are not the same as the Son's being and nature, nor the Holy Spirit's being and nature. The Father's nature is uncaused; but the Son's and the Holy Spirit's natures are caused. Noteworthy responses to Eunomius's line of reasoning came from Basil of Caesarea, his younger brother Gregory of Nyssa, and their friend Gregory of Nazianzus. (Together they are called the Cappodocian Fathers.) In working out their responses to Eunomius's arguments, they were led to articulate more clearly the distinction between "ousia" and "hypostasis." By clarifying this distinction, they found a way to undermine Eunomius's arguments and offer something of a positive account of the Trinity.

I turn to "ousia" and "hypostasis" in Section 1.3, in which I survey several accounts of the distinction between these and draw out the implications of each way of understanding the distinction. How one understands this distinction has direct implications for most other topics regarding the Trinity. So, it is important to get clear on the concept and reference of these terms. Philosophers use the phrase "intensional meaning" for a term's conceptual content, and "extensional meaning" for a term's reference. Hereafter, I use "intensional meaning" and "extensional meaning."

## 1.3 Historical Sources for Different Definitions

Trinitarian theology has several terms of art, all of which were in Greek. There were translations and interpretations of these terms in other languages, especially in Latin, Coptic, Syriac, Armenian, Arabic, and still later in modern languages. These translations typically aim to represent the meaning(s) of the Greek terms. Knowledge of the Greek terms, and debates about their meanings, is an important part of engaging with philosophical Trinitarian theology. If one were to downplay the importance of this linguistic part of Trinitarian theology, one could be led astray, at least if one accepts certain traditional criteria for articulating and evaluating an account of the Trinity. In this Element, I take Conciliar Trinitarianism as providing these traditional criteria, and use these criteria in evaluating different proposed models of the Trinity.

A *locus classicus* for identifying important terms and their meanings for Trinitarian theology is a letter, entitled "On the Difference Between *Ousia* and *Hypostasis*" (see Basil the Great 1989: 137–141). This letter was written either by Basil of Caesarea or his younger brother Gregory of Nyssa. The same letter is found in critical editions of Basil's and Gregory's writings. In Basil's writings, it is labeled *Epistle 38*; in Gregory's writings, it is labeled *To Peter*. In either case, the key distinction made in the letter is between what is common ("ousia," "phusis") and what is not common, that is, individual ("hypostasis," "prosopon") (see also Basil's *Epistle 214* and *Epistle 236*; see Basil the Great 1989: 254, 278). For example, individual human beings are the same in kind, but they are not the same individuals. What distinguishes individuals of the same kind is that each has their own noncommon characteristics. These characteristics are called "idiomata." A "hypostasis" is the term for an individual of some kind.

There is a monumental interpretive question about this letter: What is the referent of the phrase "the common nature" (*ten koinen phusis*) (see Williams 2022a: 334–339)? Is the referent the totality or collection of all individuals that *instantiate* that nature? If so, then this is a collective interpretation of "the common nature." Or is the referent one indivisible thing that exists in each and every individual of that nature? If so, then this is a distributive interpretation of "the common nature." The distributive interpretation is more likely given claims about the *indivisibility* of the one divine nature, and *numerical identity* of the one divine nature in the divine hypostases.

Gregory of Nyssa explicitly affirms in other letters that the divine nature is *indivisible* in each divine hypostasis (Gregory of Nyssa 1986: 151; 2019: 69).

The divine nature is *not numerically* different in the Father, Son, and Holy Spirit. It is numerically the same nature in each individual. This supports the distributive interpretation of "the common nature." He says:

> The Father is God, the Son is God, but by the same proclamation God is one, because neither in regard to nature nor activity is any difference viewed. If, according to the supposition of those who are mistaken, the nature in the holy Trinity has been varied, then it results that the number would extend to a quantity of gods, divided by the difference of their subjects' substance. But since the divine single and unchangeable nature rejects every difference in substance so that it would be one, it does not allow by itself a plural significance. Just as the nature is said to be one, all other aspects are named individually in the singular, God, good, holy, savior, righteous judge, and whatever other of the names befitting God comes to mind [. . .]. (Gregory of Nyssa 1986: 159)

In a passage from *On the Holy Spirit* (2011: 50; chapter 8, section 19), Basil says that the divine persons are exactly equal ("iseh") in being ("ousia"), nature ("phusis"), power ("dunamis"), and action ("energeia"), but in a subsequent passage (2011: 51; chapter 8, section 21), he quotes Jesus and comments: "'He who has seen me, has seen the Father.' He has not seen the impress or the form, for the divine nature is free from composition; he has seen however, the goodness of the will, which because it is coincident with "ousia," is considered similar and equal, or rather the same [*mallon de tauton*], in the Father and the Son." The contrast between "similar" and "the same" is between (what we would call) qualitative identity and numerical identity. Gregory of Nazianzus is clear that although there are three subjects or hypostases, they share numerically the same attributes (e.g., "light") (see 2002: 118). John of Damascus confirms the numerical identity thesis in *On the Orthodox Faith*:

> For there, that which is common and one is contemplated as an objective reality through the eternity and identity of its essence, energy, and will, and through the unanimity of its intention and the identity of its authority, power, and goodness – I did not say similarity but identity [*ouk eipon homoioteta, alla tautoteta*] – and through the one impulsion of its movement. For there is one essence, one goodness, one power, one will, one energy, one authority, one and the same, not three similar to each other, but one and the same movement of all three hypostases. (John of Damascus 2022: 80–81)

It was Gregory of Nyssa's and others' more frequent and explicit statements about the divine persons being numerically the same being ("ousia"), nature, power, and so on that were endorsed by later ecumenical councils, in particular, the sixth ecumenical council (Constantinople III) in AD 680–681 (see Williams 2022a: 343–347). I published my rediscovery of the Trinitarian theology in the sixth council in 2022 (Williams 2022a). This part of the history of Trinitarian theology is unknown to most people, including historians of theology.

As this Element makes clear, Constantinople III clarifies the Nicene-Constantinople creed, and rules out most Social models of the Trinity. This council affirmed that the divine hypostases share *numerically the same* divine nature, powers, will, and operations. In Pope St. Agatho's letter to the council (which was affirmed by the council), he claimed that it would be absurd and impious to ascribe "hypostatic wills and operations" (personal will powers and volitions) to each divine person. In another letter to the council, Pope Agatho and 125 other bishops composed a statement of faith that not only clarifies issues regarding the Incarnation, but also the Trinity. In Section 2.2, I give this statement of faith about the Trinity and derive what I take to be some essential claims of Conciliar Trinitarianism.

While Gregory of Nyssa's and Constantinople III's clarification about the Trinity are important historically and for contemporary philosophical theorizing about the Trinity, it is also important to note that such a view of the Trinity was not shared by other Christian communities who would not agree with the judgments of Constantinople III. For example, Christians who were "Miaphysites" or "Nestorians" did not endorse the claim that the divine hypostases share *numerically the same* divine nature, powers, will, and operations. They agreed that the divine hypostases are equal in divinity, power, and so on, but disagreed about numerical sameness. Most members of these groups accepted the claim that the divine hypostases have different 'idiomata' and are distinct because of these individualizing characteristics. For example, only the Father is ungenerated and generates, only the Son is generated from the Father, and only the Holy Spirit proceeds from the Father. However, "Miaphysites" like Severus of Antioch claimed that the divine nature is *divisible* into each divine hypostasis (see Severus of Antioch 2004: 85). This means that one instance of the generic divine nature is not caused (i.e., the Father), another instance of the generic divine nature is generated (i.e., the Son), and another instance of the generic divine nature proceeds from the Father (i.e., the Holy Spirit).

But, to address the unity between the divine hypostases, Severus claimed that the "whole" divine "ousia" is the Father, Son, and Holy Spirit. Severus seems to have been employing a theory of natures that is reminiscent of Porphyry of Tyre's account of universals, according to which a universal nature is the collection or totality of all individuals that participate in the same generic nature (see Williams 2019: 56–61). Each human participates in generic human nature, and human nature is the conjunction or totality of all individual human beings. Similarly, it is not uncommon in Nestorian discussions of the Trinity to say something similar, namely that "nature" refers to the total collection of individuals, and "hypostasis" refers to an individual or "singular ousia" (see Abramowski and Goodman 1972: 89, 95, 106). From this, it follows that some things are true of a part – that is, a hypostasis – that are not true of all divine hypostases. A way to understand this part–whole relation is to suppose that a part is an instantiation of a nature; a part is not the "whole nature" because the whole is the conjunction of all the parts. An instantiation of a nature is numerically distinct from any other instantiation of the same nature. By contrast, Gregory of Nyssa and Constantinople III indicate that the divine nature is not, and cannot be, divided up into numerically distinct instances, rather, it is numerically one thing in the Father, Son, and Holy Spirit. One way to put this is that it is one thing that is a constituent in each of the Father, Son, and Holy Spirit.

This difference between something that is common because it is divisible into different instantiations, and something that is common because it is a shared constituent, is a basis of competing accounts of the Trinity. Each account has prima facie strengths and weaknesses. The part–whole account (with a divisible specific nature) more easily explains how one divine hypostasis, but not another divine hypostasis, became incarnate. But the shared constituent account more easily explains another core teaching about the Trinity, namely the divine hypostases's inseparable unity of action (see Section 4.3).

Section 1.1 began by identifying a belief that Jews, Christians, and Muslims share in common, namely that there is just one God. If an account of the Trinity implies that there is more than one God, then that would be inconsistent with the traditional understanding of the Scriptures. Most Christians have said this and believed that there is just one God. However, in the mid AD 500s, there were some Christian theologians, namely some (but not all) "Miaphysites," who said and believed that each hypostasis has its own nature, that is, there are three divine natures, one for each divine hypostasis (Grillmeier 2013: 276–280; Philoponus 2017: 359–368). John Ascoutzanges proclaimed, "I confess natures, substances, and divinities according to the number of hypostases" (Van Roey and Allen 1994: 124–126; Zachhuber 2020: 156). Later, John Philoponus, who was trained in Aristotelian logic, was asked to weigh in on the discussion. He concluded that the only way for a nature to be "common" is conceptual unity, and not any real (extra-mental) unity. Since these theologians agreed that the divine nature is common to the Father, Son, and Holy Spirit, it follows that it must be divided into "particular natures." According to this Miaphysite account, a hypostasis is a "particular nature" (Zachhuber 2020: 160–167). It's an apt phrase because it signals that each hypostasis is a *part(icular)* to which the concept of the divine nature refers.

Philoponus was accused of "tri-theism," especially by Damian of Alexandria and Peter of Callinicus (see Ebied, Roey, and Wickham 1981), as well as by the sixth ecumenical council (see Williams 2022a: 350–351). Damian (so far as we know) argued that the common divine ousia was a substrate of hypostatic properties, and the hypostasis is just the property (what had been labeled an "idioma") that inheres in, or characterizes, the common substrate. On this account, a hypostasis is a property that inheres in, or characterizes, the same substrate. This is much like a Sabellian account of the Trinity according to which there is one subject or hypostasis who has three different idiomata, but it differs in that the divine subject *eternally* has these different idiomata. I call this a neo-Sabellian model of the Trinity. (An account like this is also found in the tenth-century Syriac- and Arabic-speaking Christian philosopher, Yahya Ibn 'Adi, who responded to the Muslim philosopher Al-Kindi (see Adamson 2020: 255–259, 269). Though, in a later text where Ibn 'Adi responds to Al-Warraq, he gives a different account that is similar to a Conciliar account (see Platti 1994: 183–187).) Peter of Callinicus thought Damian's account was wrong because it says that a hypostasis is identical to a property of the one divine essence. Instead, Peter contended that a hypostasis is a substrate that bears its nonshareable property, and it is a part of (or instance of) the whole divine ousia (see Zachhuber 2020: 180–181).

The foregoing history shows intense debate about how best to understand the Trinity. Most parties to this debate proclaimed the Nicene-Constantinople creed (those who didn't were, e.g., Arius, Aetius, and Eunomius), but they disagreed on the details about "hypostasis" and "ousia." Earlier, it was mentioned that one of the problems for Trinitarian theology is how to find agreement about the criteria for evaluating a model of the Trinity. If one accepts the first three ecumenical councils (Nicaea 1, Constantinople 1, and Ephesus 1), like some Miaphysites do, then one might suppose that the divine nature is divisible into three distinct *ousiai*, one instance for each divine hypostasis. But if one accepts the first six ecumenical councils (especially Constantinople III), then one might suppose that the divine nature is indivisible such that it is numerically one thing that only exists in the three divine hypostases.

## 1.4 Three Models, Three Definitions

According to Gregory of Nyssa, we should understand a hypostasis to be the subject of (i) the singular indivisible divine essence ("ousia"), nature ("phusis"), power(s) ("dunamis"), and actions ("energeia") that are common to all divine hypostases, and (ii) an unshareable hypostasis-individuating property ("idioma"). The common essence and nature is numerically one thing that is indivisible, which means that it cannot be divided into numerically distinct instances. In the language of contemporary metaphysician Peter Van Inwagen (2011), Gregory's ontology seems to be a constituent ontology and not a relational ontology. A relational ontology proposes that there are abstract universals and anything with causal powers is an instantiation of the abstract universal. It is called a relational ontology because "instantiation" (or "exemplification") is a primitive (unanalyzable) relation. A relational ontology, in this sense, proposes that concrete objects have no internal metaphysical structure, but instead a concrete object is a whole that consists of physical parts, and the physical parts are said to instantiate abstract universals. By contrast, a constituent ontology *denies* that there are abstract universals, denies this proposed primitive "instantiation" relation, and claims that concrete objects have an internal metaphysical structure that consists of metaphysical constituents. (There are different further specifications of a constituent ontology; one is that the constituents are immanent universals, another is that the constituents are tropes [individual properties].) (It seems to me that William Lane Craig mistakenly supposes that Gregory has what amounts to a relational ontology, which is why Craig seems to misunderstand Gregory's account. See Craig 2009: 89–90.)

The distinction between a relational ontology and a constituent ontology is helpful for better understanding (historical) Trinitarian theologies. Gregory of Nyssa (and Constantinople III) proposes that the divine hypostases share *numerically* the same divine being, nature, power(s), and action(s), but that these hypostases do not and cannot share other items, namely their personal properties ("idiomata"). Each of these "idioma" is a certain real relation ("skeseis") (see Anatolios 2011: 105–112; Vigorelli 2018: 538–555; Maspero 2023a). (The claim about real relations is not incidental or ad hoc; it is grounded in their exegesis of the New Testament titles and names, e.g., Father of, Son of, and Spirit of.) This ontology is an example of a constituent ontology. Each divine hypostasis's "having" the one divine nature is not an instantiation relation, but it is more like a part–whole relation according to which the singular indivisible divine nature is like an inseparable part of each and every divine hypostasis. Moreover, each divine hypostasis "has" something else that is like another inseparable part, but this other inseparable part is *not* a common or shared inseparable part with the other divine hypostases. Each divine hypostasis consists of the singular, common, divine nature, and an unshareable property that is a certain real relation (see Williams 2019: 58–59). We now have enough to articulate a Conciliar account of a divine hypostasis.

### *A Conciliar Account of a Divine Hypostasis*:

*x* is a divine hypostasis if and only if *x* is the subject of (i) the singular indivisible divine being ("ousia"), nature ("phusis"), power ("dunamis") and action ("energeia"), which are common to all divine hypostases, and (ii) an unshareable real relation to another divine hypostasis.

A second account of a divine hypostasis is given by Severus of Antioch. He was a main figure in ancient Miaphysite theology. According to Severus, we should understand a hypostasis to be a "particular nature" that has individuating characteristics, and that a hypostasis is a part of the whole totality of particular natures of the same kind. Roughly, particular natures of the same generic nature are different instances of the same generic nature. Since Severus and his followers often focus on the "whole divine nature" as consisting in three instances of the generic nature, we can say that on this proposal the generic divine nature is and can only be instantiated three times. So:

> *A Miaphysite Account of a Divine Hypostasis*:
> $x$ is a divine hypostasis if and only if $x$ is (i) a particular divine being, nature, and power who is a unique instance of the generic divine nature, and (ii) $x$ has a real relation to another divine hypostasis and nothing else whatsoever can have this real relation, and (iii) $x$ is a part of the whole totality of *particular* divine natures.

A difference between the Conciliar account and this Miaphysite account is that the mereologies are different. On the Conciliar account, a divine hypostasis is like a whole that consists of inseparable constituent parts. But on this Miaphysite account, a divine hypostasis is a part of the whole divine nature.

In contrast to these accounts of a divine hypostasis, a third account, given by, for example, Damian of Alexandria and Yahya Ibn 'Adi, has it that a divine hypostasis is a distinctive property or attribute that exists in a common subject, its "ousia." It is a common subject in the sense that three distinctive properties exist in numerically the same subject. In this proposal, there are three distinctive properties (e.g., Fatherhood, Sonship, and Procession) and each of them exists in the singular divine nature. There is no contingency involved in the proposal; so, another way to put it is that the one divine being (subject) eternally and necessarily has these three properties or attributes. Sometimes this has been labeled a Sabellian account. But the traditional Sabellian account is that the one divine nature becomes Father, Son, or Holy Spirit in relation to different interactions with the created world. However, in a proposal like Damian's and Ibn 'Adi's, it is eternally the case that the one divine nature is the Father, Son, and Holy Spirit because the attributes of Fatherhood, Sonship, and Procession eternally exist in the one divine nature. We can call the former account classic Sabellianism and this latter account neo-Sabellianism. So:

> *A Neo-Sabellian Account of a Divine Hypostasis*:
> $x$ is a divine hypostasis if and only if $x$ is (i) identical to a distinctive property that (ii) exists in numerically the same divine nature as any other distinctive property that exists in the one divine nature.

These are the three ways of defining a divine hypostasis. Each one has its historical and contemporary defenders and developers. Each one faces important clarification questions and objections. I will return to these three different definitions to show what their implications are for a given topic or challenge to Trinitarian theology.

## 1.5 Personal Pronouns

In Trinitarian theology, personal pronouns are often used to refer to a divine hypostasis or the one divine nature. It is common to find "he" used to refer to each of the divine hypostases. Oftentimes contemporary readers of Trinitarian theology bring with them contemporary concerns and debates regarding social understandings of gender or gendered pronouns. So, some use "she" to refer to the Holy Spirit to respond to contemporary concerns regarding gender or sexism.

It is important to recognize that in the context of Scripture and Trinitarian theology, it is grammatical gender that is typically in use, and not something nonlinguistic (e.g., one's self-concept of one's own gender). For example, the nouns "Father" and "Son" in Hebrew, Greek, and Latin have a masculine grammatical gender, and in turn there is a masculine personal pronoun ("he") that refers to these nouns. But the noun "Spirit" in "Holy Spirit" in Hebrew is feminine, in Greek it is neuter, and in Latin it is masculine. Furthermore, there are four passages in the *Gospel According to John* (see John 14:16–17, 15:26, 16:13–14, 17) that have the noun "Spirit" (which is neuter), but a masculine pronoun ("he") is used. A masculine pronoun is used because it refers back to an associated noun, "the Advocate," that is masculine. It would be exegetically mistaken to ask whether the Holy Spirit (the referent) is masculine, neuter, or feminine, but exegetically appropriate to ask about the grammatical gender of nouns and pronouns. Moreover, in Greek and in Latin the grammatical gender of essence ("ousia," "essentia") in "divine essence" is feminine, and not neuter. Likewise, in Greek and in Latin, the grammatical gender of "person" ("hypostasis," "persona") in "divine person" is feminine.

Given that there are nouns with different grammatical genders that may correspond to the same referent, one should avoid the incautious inference that the referent has multiple genders or just one gender. Rather, it is grammatical gender at play. Given that "hypostasis" is feminine, one could say in Greek that the first divine hypostasis is uncreated and that she is the Father. "She" would be called for because "hypostasis" is the antecedent and is grammatically feminine. By the same grammatical rules, one could also say in Greek that the divine essence includes all divine powers and that she is communicated from the

Father to the Son through the eternal generation of the Son. (There are historical examples of these kinds of sentences; see Ps.-Justin Martyr in Otto 1881: 401, 3–4.) All of this may sound confusing or ungrammatical to contemporary English speakers because English does not have grammatical genders for all nouns, grouped as either masculine, feminine, or neuter. Rather, English retains gender for what is called natural gender; pronouns like "he" and "she" have been used to refer to nonlinguistic facts.

In contemporary English, there is much discussion and debate regarding gender as social construction or requiring a self-concept. This complicates matters in discussing Trinitarian theology, just as the change of meaning of the word "person" did in the nineteenth century when it acquired the meaning of, for example, a self-conscious being (see Barth 2004: 357). Should one use "he," "she," "it," or "they" (sg. pronoun, e.g.: "Did you know that this student wrote the best paper *and* that they are an avid gardener?") when referring to God the Father, God the Son, or God the Holy Spirit? It is not evident that there is a trans-historical correct answer to this question (given different grammatical genders in different languages). What is clear is that if discussion of the Trinity is limited to discussion of texts about the Trinity that were in, for example, Greek or Latin, then one may let Greek or Latin grammatical rules determine which pronouns to use. But if one is writing in contemporary English about such texts, it is pragmatically unlikely to avoid contemporary concerns regarding the use of gendered pronouns for divine persons.

Whatever decision one makes, it seems that there are important reasons to object or raise concerns about that decision. One could try out innovations like "(t)he(y)" or "t(he)y" to indicate a singular referring pronoun, but this may be more distracting than helpful. Or one could be consistent and stipulate that it is only grammatical gender and nothing more. But for many English speakers and readers, it wouldn't feel like only grammatical gender. Another strategy would be to be overall inconsistent but in specific passages be consistent so as to minimize confusion; sometimes using "he," "she," "it," or "they" (sg.), to correspond to the same referent. This Element employs this last strategy because it is fitting given different grammatical genders (in Hebrew, Greek, or Latin) for the same referent, and fitting to the vast ontological differences between divine persons and individual human beings (see Harrison 2011: 519–530).

## 1.6 Hypostasis, Rationality, and Social Models

There is one thing that these ancient accounts of hypostasis and their historical defenders share in common. Not one of them includes in the definition of hypostasis for theorizing about the Trinity a concept of "rationality." It was Boethius (a Latin-speaking philosopher and theologian, d. 525) who added the term "rationalis" in his proposed definition of "persona" (see Williams 2019: 66–73; 2020a: 86–89). According to Boethius, a person is an individual substance of a rational nature. Although Boethius's definition of person was directly in response to questions about the incarnation of God the Son, his inclusion of rationality in his definition of person is historically significant, and significant for Trinitarian theorizing. Hence, in the Latin scholastic tradition, they distinguish a supposite (= a hypostasis of any nature) and a person (= a hypostasis of a rational nature) (see Williams 2019: 66–73). This is relevant to Trinitarian theology because *if* one supposes that being a person requires rationality, then this may (but need not) lead one to developing a Trinitarian theology that is inconsistent with Conciliar Trinitarianism. That is, one may suppose that each divine hypostasis has their own unshared rational power(s) or acts or both. This is evident in some contemporary articulations of the Trinity, usually labeled Social models, according to which a divine hypostasis (i.e., a divine person) is a "center of consciousness." Since there are three divine hypostases or persons, it follows that there are three divine centers of consciousness. If such divine hypostases are distinct from each other, then there are three distinct centers of consciousness. The claim that the divine hypostases are distinct "centers of consciousness" is inconsistent with Conciliar Trinitarianism if it entails that there are personal, unshared, acts of intellect or acts of will. For, the sixth council explicitly denies that there are any personal, unshared, operations (e.g., acts of intellect, acts of will) in the Trinity.

Another example of the contemporary trend of assuming rationality or consciousness in what a person is is found in Dale Tuggy's entry on the Trinity in the *Stanford Encyclopedia of Philosophy*. Tuggy uses the category of a "self" (i.e., a being "capable of knowledge, intentional action, and interpersonal relationships") to distinguish different theories of the Trinity. However, for those with historical sensibilities, "self" is not the relevant concept to use in Trinitarian theorizing, nor is there any historical precedent for this except after the nineteenth century when "consciousness" and "self" became a key notion in philosophy (see Barth 2004: 357). Using the term or a concept of "the self" has no theological precedent for theorizing about the Trinity. (The theological terms of art were, e.g., "nature" and "person.") This doesn't entail that it is entirely wrong to use it in Trinitarian theology, but it does mean that one must be extremely cautious, especially if one wishes to endorse a theory that is consistent with Conciliar Trinitarianism. In Section 5.3, I discuss a way in which ascribing self-knowledge to the divine hypostases is consistent with Conciliar Trinitarianism.

## 2 Hermeneutical and Logical Problems

This section summarizes some of the key claims consistent with Conciliar Trinitarianism (see Williams 2022a; Forthcoming-b). In so doing, it presents what I call the hermeneutical problem or challenge to belief in the Trinity (2.1), and the logical problem (2.3).

## 2.1 Hermeneutics

One of the fullest statements about the Trinity by an ecumenical council is in the letter from Pope St. Agatho and the 125 bishops; this letter was endorsed by the sixth ecumenical council in Constantinople. This council also endorsed the letter by Pope St. Agatho to Emperor Constantine IV. This letter to the emperor corroborates what it affirmed in the letter to the council, and it makes explicit the concern about the *numerical identity* of what the divine hypostases share in common. The summary in Section 2.2 is not meant to be exhaustive. Instead, it is meant to pick out some key sentences and common interpretations of those sentences.

One issue regarding statements by an ecumenical council is that the sentences must be interpreted. But whose interpretation? Who, if anyone, has the authority to interpret them infallibly, or at least correctly? Philosophers of religion sometimes presume that such and such a sentence must be interpreted as they interpret it. But a fairer minded approach would be to try out different interpretations and see which ones survive objection and which ones do the better job in corroborating with other sentences. It should be kept in mind that even if one interpretation survives philosophical objections, that doesn't entail that it was the understanding of those who composed the sentences that are being interpreted. There might be a fact of the matter about which interpretation is correct, but knowing if one has that interpretation is another issue. Sarah Coakley (2002) reports three ways to understanding conciliar documents and endorsed a fourth way. One way is that such statements are merely linguistic regulations or grammatical rules. Another way is that such statements are metaphorical in the sense of not making an ontological claim or having any nonlinguistic referent. A third way is that such statements are literal in the sense of precise ontological claims. Coakley contends that such statements are regulative and do make claims about reality, but they are not as precise as one today might hope. The ecumenical councils say as much as they need to, but typically do not go beyond what is required for their dialectical context(s). Later councils make clarifications, but, again, typically only to the extent required in their dialectical context(s). I agree with Coakley. In what follows, I report eleven claims that I take to be a part of Conciliar Trinitarianism. They could be made more fine-grained. But for our purposes, let them suffice.

It is helpful to recognize that Christians historically have believed that the Trinity is mysterious. One way to understand this is that we are not in a position to know which interpretations are correct, in some ahistorical way. Instead, Christians were presented with (putative) divine revelation, and have done the best they can, under divine guidance, in articulating the doctrine of the Trinity. The sentences are guides to the mystery of the Trinity, but there have been and continue to be disputes about the explanation of their meanings or entailments or both. Francisco de Vitoria (1991: 238) wrote that in theology, there are many disputes about why something is true, even if disputants agree that something is true. So, philosophers of religion, or at least philosophical theologians, can accept (as true, or for the sake of argument) certain sentences but dispute why they are true (or how they could be true). That is, a sentence is true (or could be true), given such and such an interpretation of the sentence. The interpretations of the following sentences about the Trinity have been, and continue to be, disputed (see Jedwab and Keller 2019). Given all this, it follows that if there is a logical inconsistency between certain sentences, then it is likely that it is the interpretation of the sentences that faces logical inconsistency. Call this a local defeater for belief in Conciliar Trinitarianism. But if all possible interpretations of the sentences turn out to be logically inconsistent, then the logical problem would be an all-interpretations-considered defeater for belief in Conciliar Trinitarianism. (At least, this is so unless one accepts divine contradictions like Jc Beall (2023). See near the end of Section 2.3 for a discussion of Beall's account.)

## 2.2 Conciliar Trinitarianism

The sixth ecumenical council endorsed the letter composed in Greek by Pope St. Agatho and the 125 bishops. The section on the Trinity says:

> We believe in one God, the Father Almighty, maker of heaven and earth, and of all things visible and invisible; and in his only-begotten Son, who was begotten of him before all worlds; true God from God, Light from Light, begotten not made, co-essential [*homoousion*] with the Father, that is of the very same essence [*ousias*] with the Father; through him were all things made which are in heaven and which are on earth; and in the Holy Spirit, the Lord and giver of life, who proceeds from the Father, and with the Father and Son together is worshiped and glorified; the Trinity in unity and unity in the Trinity; a unity of essence [*ousias*] but a trinity of prosopa or hypostases; and so we confess God the Father, God the Son, and God the Holy Spirit; not three gods, but one God, the Father, the Son, and the Holy Spirit; not a hypostasis of three names, but one essence of

three hypostases [*trion hypostaseon mian ousian*], thus one essence and nature, that is to say one deity, one eternity, one power, one kingdom, one glory, one adoration, one essential will and operation of the same Holy and inseparable Trinity [*hen ousiodes tes autes agias kai akoristou triados thelema kai energeia*], which ha[s] created all things, ha[s] made disposition of them, and still contains them. (Percival 1988: 340, with slight changes by me)

In the letter addressed to Emperor Constantine IV, Pope Agatho says:

This then is the status of our evangelical and Apostolic faith, to wit, that as we confess the holy and inseparable Trinity, that is, the Father, the Son, and the Holy Spirit, to be [*einai*] of one deity, of one nature and essence, so we will profess also that it has one natural will, power, operation, domination, majesty, potency, and glory. And whatever is said of the same Holy Trinity essentially in singular number [*henikoi arithmoi*] we apprehend [*katalambanometha*] as from the one nature of the three co- essential prosopa, having been so taught by canonical logic [*kanonikoi logoi*]. (Percival 1988: 330, with slight changes by me)

And:

Consequently, therefore, according to the rule of the holy Catholic and Apostolic Church of Christ, she also confesses and preaches that there are in [Christ] two natural wills and two natural operations. For if anybody should mean a personal will [*hean gar tis prosopikon noesei to thelema*], when in the holy Trinity there are said to be three persons [*prosopa*], it would be necessary that there should be asserted three personal wills and three personal operations [*tria prosopika thelemata kai treis prosopikas energeias*] (which is absurd and truly profane). Since, as the truth of the Christian faith holds, the will is natural, where the one nature of the holy and inseparable Trinity is spoken of, it must be consistently understood that there is one natural will and one natural operation [*hen phusikon thelema kai mia phusike energeia*]. (Percival 1988: 332–333)

There is one background claim (which I represent as claim (1)) that needs to be made explicit. All participants in the sixth ecumenical council, in accordance with all of the accepted theological authorities, believed that God the Father is the *uncaused* divine hypostasis (see Branson 2022: 20–29). I assume this in my summary, while recognizing that it is not explicit in the statements quoted from Constantinople III. If anyone doubts the credentials of this claim about God the Father, then they would be in the extreme minority. So, here is one way to distil some key claims from these statements of faith about the Trinity:

### Summary Interpretation of Constantinople III

1. There is one uncaused divine hypostasis.
2. There is one divine hypostasis who is generated from the uncaused divine hypostasis.
3. There is one divine hypostasis who proceeds from the uncaused divine hypostasis.
4. It is not the case that there is one divine hypostasis who is the Father, Son, and Holy Spirit. [*Contra* Sabellianism]
5. There are three divine hypostases.
6. The uncaused divine hypostasis is neither the generated hypostasis nor the hypostasis who proceeds, nor vice versa.
7. The three divine hypostases share numerically the same divine essence and nature. [*Contra* the Miaphysite three-instantiation model, and Arianism]
8. There is one God because the uncaused divine hypostasis shares *numerically the same* divine essence and nature with the generated hypostasis and with the hypostasis who proceeds.
9. The three divine hypostases share numerically the same power(s), will, and operation(s). [*Contra* the Miaphysite three-instantiation model, and Arianism]

Constantinople III endorsed the previous five ecumenical councils' judgments. This includes Nicaea I's condemnation of Arius's account of how the Father and Son relate to each other. That council rejected the claim that there was a time when the Son was not, and it rejected the claim that the Son is of a different, lesser *being* than the Father (see Tanner 1990: 5). For, the council affirmed that the Father and Son are the same being (*homoousion*). These two denials are repeated in Sophronius of Jerusalem's *Synodical Letter*, which was read aloud and solemnly affirmed by Constantinople III (Williams 2022a: 340, 349–352). So,

10. There was not a time at which there was no divine hypostasis who is the Son.
11. The three divine hypostases are not different in essence and nature.

## 2.3 The Logical Problem

It is not immediately evident where a prima facie logical inconsistency may be found in (1)–(11). Clarification questions would help in locating a logical inconsistency. Perhaps the most relevant question is, "what is the relation between a divine hypostasis and the one divine nature?" Is it numerical identity (e.g., "The Father is numerically identical to God")? Is it predication (e.g., "The Father is divine")? Or some other relation? These are the kinds of questions for which philosophers would like answers. Unfortunately, the creedal statement does not give specific enough guidance for which precise option, or options, one should go with, particularly in light of contemporary studies in logic. So, what a philosopher can do is argue that if the logical relation is such and such, then here is the implication. If an implication is a logical inconsistency, then that is the logical problem for belief in the Trinity. What a believer in the Trinity should be aware of is that the creed itself does not explicitly commit one to a precise (or, fine-grained) determinate answer to the question about the logical relation between "a divine hypostasis" and "the divine nature." Philosophers and theologians working on the logical problem must be mindful of the hermeneutical context; otherwise, they might mistake success (one way or the other) as final success. As Gregory of Nazianzus would put it, the revelation of the Trinity was to fishermen, not to trained Aristotelians (see Grillmeier 1975a; Gregory of Nazianzus 2003: 140). Nevertheless, some interpretations are more promising than others because they do not imply logical inconsistency and cohere with various theological authorities (e.g., Scripture, the ecumenical councils, respected theologians).

One of the classic analytical treatments of the "logical problem of the Trinity" in the twentieth century was by Richard Cartwright. He made explicit reference to the Pseudo-Athanasian creed to get sentences that are more easily amenable to logical analysis. The content of the Pseudo-Athanasian creed overlaps in some, but not all, ways with the conciliar statements from Constantinople III (see Williams 2022a: 354–356). According to Cartwright (1987: 188), the logical problem of the Trinity shows up in the following sentences:

### Summary of the Pseudo-Athanasian Creed

1. The Father is God.
2. The Son is God.
3. The Holy Spirit is God.
4. The Father isn't the Son.
5. The Father isn't the Holy Spirit.
6. The Son isn't the Holy Spirit.
7. There is only one God.

This presentation invites investigation into logical relations, and especially whether the logical relation of inconsistency is entailed by the conjunction of these sentences. It seems that (1)–(7) are logically inconsistent. How could the Father, Son, and Holy Spirit be the same God, and yet not be the same as each other? Note that these sentences do not mention or use the term "hypostasis" or "person." The Pseudo-Athanasian creed does say that the Father is a person, the Son is a person, and the Holy Spirit is a person, and that they are not the same person. Like Constantinople III, the Pseudo-Athanasian creed also makes claims about causal relations between these divine persons. But Cartwright's summary does not include these claims. Consequently, this summary does not represent some key claims of Conciliar Trinitarianism. (One consequence of this way of summarizing claims about the Trinity is that it may tempt its readers to try to resolve the apparent logical inconsistency by supposing that the causal relations between the hypostases are not, in fact, an essential part of Conciliar Trinitarianism.)

Nevertheless, engaging with this summary may be useful for two reasons. First, if there is a logical inconsistency, this may show it. Second, it motivates one to wrestle with an important question: What is the relation between a divine hypostasis and the one divine nature? One way to avoid logical inconsistency would be to go with a Miaphysite three-instantiation model. (Note: not all historical Miaphysites endorsed this model [see Van Roey and Allen 1994: 126–129].) Assuming this model, we would gloss this summary as follows:

### Three-Instantiation Gloss of the Summary of the Pseudo-Athanasian Creed

1'. The Father is divine (*by instantiating* the divine nature).
2'. The Son is divine (*by instantiating* the divine nature).
3'. The Holy Spirit is divine (*by instantiating* the divine nature).
4'. The Father is not numerically identical to the Son.
5'. The Father is not numerically identical to the Holy Spirit.
6'. The Son is not numerically identical to the Holy Spirit.
7'. There is only one instantiable divine nature.

This interpretation avoids logical inconsistency by proposing that the divine nature is like an abstract nature that is instantiated three times, one instantiation for each divine hypostasis. The relation between each divine hypostasis and the divine nature is expressed by predication (see Wierenga 2004: 288–290). Although this gloss avoids internal logical inconsistency, it is not consistent with Conciliar Trinitarianism. For, according to Conciliar Trinitarianism, there is only numerically one divine nature and not three numerically distinct instances of it. The numerically one divine nature is communicated from the Father to the Son, and from the Father to the Holy Spirit. The general problem is that the Miaphysite three-instantiation model assumes an instantiation relation (from concrete object to the abstract universal), while the Conciliar model is inconsistent with any such instantiation relation.

Peter Van Inwagen (2009, 2022) makes use of the logic of relative identity to show that a traditional Trinitarian can interpret the Pseudo-Athanasian creed without entailing any logical contradiction. This proposal says that sameness is relative to a sortal. So, the divine persons are the same God as each other, but they are not the same person as each other. In this account, identity is relative to a sortal. Suppose that "God" is a sortal term, and "person" is a sortal term. So, the Father, Son, and the Holy Spirit are the same regarding the sortal "God," but they are not the same with regard to the sortal "person." This use of relative identity addresses the logical problem that Cartwright raises, but it leaves the Trinitarian wondering about the ontology. The appeal to relative identity is a defensive strategy in response to the logical problem. As a mere defense against this logical problem, it seems plausible. But, as an account of the Trinity, even one limited to Conciliar Trinitarianism, it is underdeveloped.

Another way to respond to the Summary of the Pseudo-Athanasian Creed, and the question "what is the relation between a divine hypostasis and the divine nature?" is to use a notion of numerical sameness without identity. Jeffrey Brower and Michael Rea (2005) introduced this relation into contemporary discourse about the Trinity. (However, there are some medieval antecedents; see Brower 2004; Williams 2012.) According to them, numerical sameness without identity is not predication, because predication implies numerical distinction. (For example, Socrates is a human, Plato is a human, and Socrates's individual human nature is not numerically identical to Plato's individual human nature.) Nor is it numerical *identity* because although a numerical relation obtains, classical identity doesn't obtain. To illustrate this, they give the example of a statue and the material from which it is made. Consider a bronze statue of Athena and the lump of bronze from which it is made. The statue of Athena is numerically the same material object as this lump of bronze. But the bronze statue is not identical to the lump of bronze because some things are true of the bronze statue but are not true of the lump of bronze. For, the lump of bronze existed prior to the bronze statue of Athena, and the bronze statue of Athena can be destroyed while the same lump of bronze continues to exist. This indicates that the lump of bronze and the bronze statue of Athena do not have the same persistence conditions, nor the same modal properties. Hence, the bronze statue of Athena is numerically the same material object as the lump of bronze, but the bronze statue of Athena is not identical to this lump of bronze. In the case of classical numerical identity, whatever is true of $a$ is true of $b$, and vice versa, and the relation is symmetric and transitive. But in the case of numerical sameness without identity, it is not the case that whatever is true of $a$ is true of $b$, and vice versa. Nevertheless, this relation also is symmetric and transitive (2005: 74, n. 1). Hence, if the bronze statue of Athena is numerically the same material object as the lump of bronze without identity, then (by symmetry) the lump of bronze is numerically the same material object as the bronze statue of Athena without identity. If there were a creative artist who made three statues out of numerically the same lump of bronze at the same time, then these three statues would be numerically the same material object as each other, *and* they'd be numerically the same lump of bronze, and none would be identical to each other.

Brower and Rea apply these considerations to the Trinity. Each divine hypostasis is like the bronze statue of Athena, and the divine nature is like the lump of bronze. The divine nature (like the bronze that instantiates the statue of Athena) instantiates three different properties, *being a Father*, *being a Son*, and *being a Spirit* (Brower and Rea 2005: 68). A divine hypostasis is numerically the same immaterial object as the one divine nature without being identical to the one divine nature. There is no numerical *identity* between the one divine nature and a divine hypostasis because the one divine nature is shared among the three divine hypostases, but no divine hypostasis is shared with anything else. The divine hypostases are distinct from each other because of their nonshared personal properties. In the case of the statue of Athena and the lump of bronze, the relation is *contingent* numerical sameness without identity. But in the case of the divine hypostases and the divine nature, the relation is *essential* numerical sameness without identity (ENSWI). This implies that a divine hypostasis exists only if it is numerically the same immaterial object as the one divine nature without being identical to it, and vice versa. (If we assume that each divine hypostasis is a necessary being, then the relation is *necessary* numerical sameness without identity.)

Several informative objections have been raised against this example that illustrates the relation of numerical sameness without identity. One is a clarification question: What is the "immaterial object" to which each divine hypostasis is numerically the same (see Craig 2005)? If it is a vague object, or an ambiguous object, then if vagueness and ambiguity are features of language or epistemology, then there *is no* such mind- or language-independent vague or ambiguous object. Hence, there is not a thing to which a divine hypostasis is numerically the same as without being identical to it. It would seem that the items in relation to one another are each divine hypostasis and the one divine nature. If the "immaterial object" is no thing in addition to these, then it is better to omit the phrase. But if the phrase is omitted, then there is no term that refers to that in which the divine hypostases are numerically the same without identity.

Another objection asks: Why suppose that a divine hypostasis's personal property is like a form that characterizes the divine nature? After all, the Conciliar view claims that a personal property doesn't characterize the divine nature but rather a divine hypostasis. If a personal property were said to characterize the divine nature, then that would imply a kind of Sabellianism, according to which there is one hypostasis (the divine nature) who has the characteristic of being the Father, Son, and Holy Spirit (see Pruss 2009: 317–318).

These worries are persuasive regarding *how* Rea and Brower articulate numerical sameness without identity in regard to the Trinity. One way to resolve these worries and maintain the thesis that each divine hypostasis is essentially numerically the same *something* as the divine nature without being identical to it is to reject the analogy of a divine hypostasis being like a hylomorphic compound according to which a form characterizes matter. Instead, as suggested by, for example, Henry of Ghent (see Williams 2012: 139–142) and John Duns Scotus (see Paasch 2012: 67–77), suppose that each divine hypostasis is constituted by a personal relation and the one divine nature. Unlike Brower and Rea's model, this proposal has it that the one divine nature is not characterized by a personal relation (e.g., *being Father of*), but instead, a hypostasis is characterized by a personal relation. This adjustment removes the suggestion that the one divine nature instantiates or is characterized by any personal relation. Instead of implying that the one divine nature is the Father of the Son (by instantiating the "father of" relation), this proposal is that the Father is the Father of the Son.

In this different (medieval) account, each divine hypostasis has (at least) two constituents: the one divine nature and a personal property. There is not a vague or ambiguous "immaterial object" that is in addition to the divine hypostases, their "idiomata," and the one divine nature. Still, the divine hypostases share numerically the same divine nature as each other, and none of the hypostases are numerically identical to the one divine nature. It is important to get clear on what is meant about the one divine nature. The divine nature is a concrete entity that has an existence condition, namely, it is a *constituent* of a divine hypostasis. It exists as a constituent of the uncaused divine hypostasis who (eternally) communicates it to (or shares it with) the second divine hypostasis through generating that hypostasis. Similarly, the uncaused divine hypostasis (eternally) communicates it to (or shares it with) the third divine hypostasis through spirating that hypostasis. (Gregory of Nyssa, and many others, argued that a common nature only exists in a hypostasis or in hypostases. There is no common nature that exists apart from a hypostasis (see Erismann 2010: 75–91). So, there is no abstract universal called "the divine nature.") This existence condition for the one divine nature is explained by the (proposed) fact that a divine hypostasis is essentially (and necessarily) numerically the same divine nature as the one divine nature, without being identical to the one divine nature. This relation is symmetrical and transitive, but the overall account differs from Brower and Rea's account because of a different background account of how each personal property conjoins to the one divine nature. Brower and Rea say that the divine nature is characterized by each of them. Ghent and Scotus say that each hypostasis is characterized by a personal property and not the one divine nature. I abbreviate this relation as "ENSWI."

How then can ENSWI be used to interpret the Summary of the Pseudo-Athanasian Creed? It depends in part on how the term "God" is used. The term "God" can be used with indefinite reference to a certain divine hypostasis. Hence, "God" refers to the conjunction of the one (trope of the) divine nature and a hypostasis (see Basil the Great 1989: 278). (By "trope," I mean an individual concrete property.) Another meaning is that "God" is used to refer to the one (trope of the) divine nature (John of Damascus 2022: 171). A third meaning is that "God" is used to refer to divine activity (Gregory of Nyssa 1986: 153). For the sake of this example, let's assume that "God" refers to the one divine nature.

**ENSWI Interpretation of the Pseudo-Athanasian Creed, "God" -> the one divine nature**

1". The Father is (essentially numerically the same divine nature as) the one divine nature without being identical to it.

2". The Son is (essentially numerically the same divine nature as) the one divine nature without being identical to it.

3". The Holy Spirit is (essentially numerically the same divine nature as) the one divine nature without being identical to it.

4'. The Father is not numerically identical to the Son.

5'. The Father is not numerically identical to the Holy Spirit.

6'. The Son is not numerically identical to the Holy Spirit.

7". There is only one (trope of the) divine nature and it only exists in the Father, Son, and Holy Spirit.

What follows from these claims is that the divine hypostases share numerically the same divine nature, and none of the hypostases are identical to it, nor to each other. These claims are logically consistent with each other, and so there is no logical contradiction.

Jc Beall's take on the logical problem is to deny that statements like "the Father is God" and "the Son is God," are to be interpreted as *classical* identity statements (Beall 2023: 8). According to classical identity, $a$ is identical to $b$ if and only if the relation between $a$ and $b$ is reflexive, symmetrical, *and* transitive. So, if $a$ is (classically identical to) $b$, then by symmetry it follows that $b$ is $a$. And, by transitivity, it follows that if $a$ is $b$, and $b$ is $c$, then $a$ is $c$. Beall agrees that the relation expressed by "the Father is God," is reflexive and symmetrical but denies that it is transitive. This implies that the statements that "the Father is God," "the Son is God," and "there is only one God," do not jointly entail (or have as a logical consequence) that "the Father is the Son." For them to entail that "the Father is the Son," would require a consequence by transitivity. But, since there is no such transitivity, according to Beall, it doesn't follow from these statements that "the Father is the

Son." Furthermore, Beall contends that there are true contradictions said of the "triune God." He argues that classical identity, while perhaps true in some domains of reality, need not be true in all domains of reality, particularly in the domain of the triune God. Beall states that:

> To say that Father begot Son is to speak truly – with no contradiction. To say that Father is God is to speak truly – a fundamental, axiomatic truth – but the identity is also false; for the Spirit is God and it's just false that the Spirit begot the Son. That Spirit is God is true – fundamentally, axiomatically true – but also false; for Christ is God and Christ is begotten, but it's just false that the Spirit is begotten. The contradictions are natural but only salient when talking "across" trinitarian reality. (Beall 2023: 39)

In brief, Beall affirms that God is the Father, God is the Son, God became incarnate, *and* it is false that God became incarnate. The last two statements are contradictory; but to save the known truths about the Trinity, we must accept this as a case of a true contradiction.

There are several concerns for Beall's response to the logical problem. First, he is content to say that all divine persons are identical to God (without transitivity). What is worrisome about this proposal is that it appears to be a version of Sabellianism, according to which there is just one divine hypostasis, God, who is (eternally identical to) the Father, Son, and Holy Spirit. A more precise way to put the worry is the following. Beall contends that "the Father is God" expresses a relation that is symmetrical, so that it entails "God is the Father." However, neither the Pseudo-Athanasian creed nor Constantinople III endorses the latter claim. Instead, both affirm the former statement, and Constantinople III is incompatible with the inference by symmetry to the second statement. For, according to Constantinople III, there is "one God" because there is "one essence of three hypostases." The one divine essence is said of the three hypostases, but Constantinople III denies that three hypostases are said of (or names) the one divine essence. The Sabellian move is to affirm that there is "one hypostasis of three names." And that is equivalent to what Beall endorses by affirming that symmetry obtains in "the Father is God," so as to justify the immediate inference to "God is the Father."

The "Logical Problem of the Trinity" typically arises when the term "God" is used with the same intension and extension in different sentences, such that the conjunction of sentences is interpreted to imply that there is only one God *and* there are three Gods. From the perspective of Conciliar Trinitarianism, we must be cautious about how the term "God" (*Theos, Deus*) is used. In the creedal statement from Constantinople III, we read:

**Constantinople III: Select Statements 1**

1  We confess [. . .] God the Father, God the Son, and God the Holy Spirit;
2  not three gods,
3  but one God, the Father, the Son, and the Holy Spirit;
4  not a hypostasis of three names, but one essence of three hypostases.

Note that there are different uses of the term "God." In line 1, "God" is said of each divine hypostasis. I take the meaning of "God" in line 1 to be "a divine hypostasis." So, the proposed clarification of this is: "[W]e confess a divine hypostasis who is the Father, a divine hypostasis who is the Son, and a divine hypostasis who is the Holy Spirit." In line 2, we have "not three gods." "God(s)" here refers to the number of divine natures. The denial is that there are not three instances (or three tropes) of the one divine nature. I think this is the right interpretation because of the explanation of "one God" that is given in line 4. In line 3, "God" refers to the one divine essence (or nature) because in the subsequent clause it is explained that there is "one God" because there is "one essence." So, the denial in line 2 is plausibly interpreted as the denial of three instances (or three tropes) of the divine nature. (This is precisely how Gregory of Nyssa contrasts the difference between "one God" and "many Gods": The difference has to do with the number of divine natures. See Gregory of Nyssa 2019: 62–63.)

The upshot of this exegesis of Constantinople III is that the relation between a divine hypostasis and the one divine nature is *not* symmetrical. This, then, is also a problem for Brower and Rea's numerical sameness without identity, since their proposed relation is symmetric and transitive. If ENSWI were an asymmetrical relation, then 1", 2", and 3" each would *not* entail a converse statement. One couldn't infer from "the Father is [ENSWI] God" to "God is [ENSWI] the Father." It may be hard to see why this would be a problem. But we can see the problem by considering the following. If we suppose that the divine nature is numerically the same as the Father without identity to the Father, then it is consistent with this view that the divine nature is the subject of the Father of relation, and, hence, this would be the illicit (neo-)Sabellian view. Asymmetry rules this out and gives us what Constantinople III teaches (more on asymmetry in what follows).

Much of Beall's dialectic depends on the assumption that we should interpret the Pseudo-Athanasian creed in the most straightforward "flat-footed" way. For Beall, the straightforward interpretation is identity (without transitivity). By limiting himself to this creed, Beall doesn't avail himself of further resources from an ecumenically endorsed statement about the Trinity, namely from Constantinople III. If he had, he would be forced to accept that the term "God" is used in different ways such that sometimes its intension is "a certain divine hypostasis" and its extension is the Father, Son, or Holy Spirit; and sometimes its intension is "the one divine nature" and its extension is just the one divine nature. Without this clarification, Beall (mistakenly) supposes that *being divine* is identical to *being God*. But that's misleading, given Conciliar Trinitarianism. For, "divinity" refers to the one divine nature (that is common to the divine hypostases), and the name "God" can refer either to the one divine nature or, distributively, to the Father, Son, or Holy Spirit, or to divine activity. "God" is not the name for a hypostasis who bears all of the incommunicable personal properties (*being Father*, *being Son*, and *being Holy Spirit*), as Beall suggests. (For other worries regarding Jc Beall's contradictory theology, see Page 2021.)

What the foregoing shows is that the relation between "a divine hypostasis" and "the one divine nature" is asymmetrical. But this also shows that there is just one divine nature. There is no abstract universal nature that is instantiated once, or three times. There is just numerically one concrete divine nature. Let's call this a trope of the divine nature. (A trope is an individual concrete being or entity; there can be a trope of a nature, of an action, etc.) This trope of the divine nature is a constituent of each and every divine hypostasis. A standard relation that is asymmetrical is predication. For example, "Perpetua is a human being" and "Felicity is a human being." Being human is predicated of Perpetua, but Perpetua is not identical to being human. If she were, then Perpetua's trope of human nature would be Felicity's trope human nature. But they are numerically different human beings. The same specific nature (human nature) is predicated of Perpetua and Felicity, but not numerically the same trope of human nature is predicated of Perpetua and Felicity. This kind of relation may be labeled "specific predication." Specific predication expresses an asymmetrical relation, *and* it implies that, for example, Perpetua's trope of human nature is not numerically identical to Felicity's trope of human nature. If specific predication were expressed in the statements "the Father is God" and "the Son is God," then each would be divine, but the Father's trope of divinity would not be numerically identical to the Son's trope of divinity.

What is needed to avoid the logical problem of the Trinity *and* be consistent with Conciliar Trinitarianism is to say that the relation is not *specific* predication, but rather *numerical* predication. In the case of the Trinity, numerical predication is a certain relation between a divine hypostasis and the one trope of the divine nature. This relation is asymmetrical, *and* the one trope of the divine nature is numerically the same trope in all divine hypostases. Numerical predication is not only asymmetrical but also transitive. Sentences like "the Father is the one divine nature," "the Son is the one divine nature," and "the Holy Spirit is the one divine nature" each express numerical predication. So, if the Father is the one trope of the divine nature and the Son is the one trope of the divine nature, then the

Father's trope of the divine nature and the Son's trope of the divine nature are numerically the same trope. Moreover, if the Son is the one trope of the divine nature and the Holy Spirit is the one trope of the divine nature, then (by transitivity) the Father's trope of the one divine nature is numerically the same trope as the Holy Spirit's trope of the one divine nature. Numerical predication avoids the implication that there are three tropes of the divine nature (or three gods) because of the numerical sameness of the Father's trope of the divine nature, the Son's trope of the divine nature, and the Holy Spirit's trope of the divine nature. Moreover, numerical predication avoids the logical consequence that the Father is the Son because no divine hypostasis is numerically identical to the one trope of the divine nature. For, the one trope of the divine nature is predicated of each and every divine hypostasis, but not vice versa.

A feature of predication is that what is in the predicate position is somehow more general than what is in the subject position. It is evident from Constantinople III and theologians like Basil the Great and Gregory of Nyssa that the one divine nature is "common," and the divine hypostases are not common (see Basil the Great 1989: 137, which is *Epistle 38*). Given that the one divine nature is common to the Father, Son, and Holy Spirit, and a divine hypostasis is not common to another divine hypostasis, predication (asymmetry) expresses how the common thing is related to each divine hypostasis. And *numerical* predication implies that the referent of the predicate in the different sentences is numerically the same (unlike specific predication that implies numerical difference).

### Numerical Predication Interpretation of the Pseudo-Athanasian Creed, "God" -> the one divine nature

1'''. The Father is divine (by having the one divine nature as a constituent).

2'''. The Son is divine (by having the one divine nature as a constituent).

3'''. The Holy Spirit is divine (by having the one divine nature as a constituent).

4'. The Father is not numerically identical to the Son.

5'. The Father is not numerically identical to the Holy Spirit.

6'. The Son is not numerically identical to the Holy Spirit.

7''. There is only one (trope of the) divine nature and it only exists in the Father, Son, and Holy Spirit.

It is important to note that 7'' expresses the implication of numerical predication in asserting that there is only one trope of the divine nature. The Father's divine nature, the Son's divine nature, and the Holy Spirit's divine nature are numerically identical. But no divine hypostasis is numerically identical to the one divine nature (since the relation is asymmetrical, and not symmetrical), nor is any divine hypostasis numerically identical to another divine hypostasis (since they do not share all the same constituents, they have different "idiomata").

## 3 Monarchy, Equality, and the *Filioque*

### 3.1 Monarchy

The Nicene-Constantinople creed begins by proclaiming that there is "one God, the Father, creator of all things visible and invisible [. . .]." The relation between the "one God" and the "Father" is very close. Moreover, the Son is "God from God [. . .], generated, not made, of the same essence as the Father," and the Holy Spirit "proceeds from the Father, and together with the Father and Son is worshiped and glorified." The Father is traditionally said to be the "one God" and the Son and Holy Spirit are understood to be from the Father (see Lombardo 2022). Gregory of Nyssa, among others, claims that there is a monarchy in the Trinity because the Father communicates *numerically the same divine nature*, which the Father is (given numerical predication), to the Son and to Holy Spirit. If one were to claim that the divine nature is "partitioned" into numerically distinct instances, then one denies the monarchy and affirms polytheism (see Gregory of Nyssa: 2019: 69). "Monarchy" means "one" (*monos*) "power" or "principle" (*arche*). If one were to posit a plurality of divine powers, namely one set of divine powers for each divine hypostasis, then there would not be a monarchy but a polyarchy. There would be three Gods, and not one God. For Gregory and many others, what secures the fact that the Son and the Holy Spirit share numerically the same divine powers is that each is from the very same divine hypostasis, the Father. The Father is the uncaused cause of the other divine hypostases (see Batillo 2018; DelCogliano 2010). As Gregory of Nazianzus (2003: 111) and Gregory Palamas (2022: 107, 125) might put it, the monarchy of the Father consists in the conjunction of three claims. First, the Father is uncaused. Second, the Father alone (eternally) causes the Son and the Holy Spirit. Third, the Son and the Holy Spirit share numerically the same divine nature as the Father's divine nature because the Father communicates it to them. If the "monarchy of the Father" consists of these three claims, then it is consistent with Conciliar Trinitarianism.

However, some philosophical theologians reject the second claim on the assumption that to be a *divine* hypostasis requires that the hypostasis is uncaused. Hence, neither the Son nor the Holy Spirit are (said to be) in any sense caused (see Hasker 2013: 214–225; 2023; Mullins 2023). Gregory of Nyssa (1986: 160) and others gave a traditional response to this kind of objection. He distinguishes the Father's nature, and how the Father has this nature. The Father, as a hypostasis, is uncaused. This attribute of being uncaused is traditionally called an "idioma" or personal property. But the Father as a *divine* hypostasis "is" in some sense the divine nature (e.g., numerical predication) (see Section 2.3). If a certain non-identity relation is plausible, then the Son can share the Father's divine nature and not share the Father's *being uncaused*, because being an uncaused hypostasis is not an "idioma" of the divine nature. The Son has a different "idioma," namely *being generated* from the Father. And, the Holy Spirit has a still different "idioma," namely the hypostasis who *proceeds* from the Father.

## 3.2 The One God

In the history of Trinitarian theology, we find that the claim that the "Father is the one God" is common (see Branson: 2022: 24–44). The Nicene creed begins with, "We believe in one God, the Father [. . .]." But what is the relation between the "one God" and "the Father"? Some philosophical theologians wonder if this relation is classical identity. Identity in this sense is numerical identity, as opposed to qualitative identity. If "the Father is the one God" is a numerical identity statement, then it follows (by symmetry) that "the one God is the Father." Moreover, if it is a numerical identity statement, then whatever is true of the one God is true of the Father, and vice versa.

Conciliar Trinitarianism does not specify by way of a fine-grained analysis what the relation is between the "one God" and "the Father." It seems to be an open question in the context of Conciliar Trinitarianism. For example, Beau Branson (an Eastern Orthodox philosophical theologian) suggests that in certain linguistic contexts, the relation be understood as numerical identity (2022: 24). At least, if one says, "the one God is the Father," and vice versa, the reason why one says this (or should say this) is that the Father is the uncaused divine hypostasis. On such an occasion, one uses the term "God" to refer only to the Father. It's a name for the Father in that context of use. In such a linguistic context, the sentence should be understood as a numerical identity statement. Joshua Sijuwade also claims that the relation is numerical identity (2022). Sijuwade is a Roman Catholic. And Dale Tuggy also contends that God is numerically identical to the Father (2021b). Tuggy is a Unitarian Christian.

As pointed out in Section 2.3, the term "God" is used to mean different things. Either it can be used to refer to the one divine nature, a divine hypostasis, or to divine activity. So, if someone says that "the Father is the one God," then it is important to understand what is being said. Does "God" in this use of the term imply that the divine essence is predicated of the Father? Or does it imply that the description "being a divine hypostasis" is predicated of the Father? Or does it predicate divine activity of the Father? Or does it say that the Father is numerically identical to the one divine nature? It is important, if possible, to get some guidance on how best to understand the statement "the Father is the one God." Fortunately, we find guidance from Constantinople III's statements about the Trinity. Consider the following select statements from Constantinople III:

### Constantinople III: Select Statements 2

1  We believe in one God, the Father Almighty [. . .],
2  [. . .] God the Father, God the Son, and God the Holy Spirit;
3  not three gods,
4  but one God, the Father, the Son, and the Holy Spirit;
5  not a hypostasis of three names, but one essence of three hypostases.

In line 2, the term "God" means a divine hypostasis. So, "a divine hypostasis, the Father; a divine hypostasis, the Son; and a divine hypostasis, the Holy Spirit." In line 4, the term "God" refers to the one (trope of the) divine essence (or nature). This is explained in line 5; "one God" refers to "one essence" that is "of three hypostases." Now the question is: What is the meaning of "one God" in line 1? I think the most plausible interpretation is to suppose that it has to do with the monarchy of the Father. Recall that "monarchy of the Father" includes three claims: The Father is the uncaused divine hypostasis, the Father (eternally) causes the Son and the Holy Spirit, and the Father communicates numerically the same divine nature to the Son (through generating the Son) and Holy Spirit (through spirating the Holy Spirit). There is "one God" because of these three things. This explains why the statement is made. But it remains to be seen what the relation is between "the Father" and the "one God." Given the discussion of Constantinople III in Sections 2.2 and 2.3, this is best understood as a relation that is not numerical identity but something else, namely numerical predication. If it is numerical predication, then "the Father is the one God" means that the "Father is divine" (assuming that the one (trope of the) divine nature is a constituent of the Father). Whatever explanation one goes with, the *reason* for making the claim that "the Father is the one God" is the Father's monarchy. The reason why the creed makes this statement is to teach us something about God the Father, namely that the Father is the uncaused divine hypostasis, the Father causes the Son and the Holy Spirit, and the Father communicates numerically the same divine nature to the Son (through eternal generation) and to the Holy Spirit (through eternal spiration). That, in a nutshell, is the conversational implication of the opening line of the Nicene-Constantinople creed.

There is a way to explain this special statement that the "Father is the one God," namely by the hermeneutical doctrine of appropriation. According to the doctrine of appropriation, in a social situation in which someone does not understand much about the Trinity, a theologian may appropriate one attribute that is shared in common by the divine hypostases and associate it with just one divine hypostasis, and do the same for the other two divine hypostases. This linguistic practice is especially clear in the New Testament's *Epistle to the Hebrews*; Biblical scholars call this "prosopological exegesis" – "prosopa" is a Greek term for person (see Pierce 2020). So, a theologian may say "the Father is divine power, the Son is divine wisdom, and the Holy Spirit is divine love." This triad of statements is meant to teach something about the Trinity. For example, it can teach that there are three hypostases and that there is some sort of order between them. If someone grasps these points through this appropriation of common attributes (power, wisdom, love) to certain divine hypostases, then the theologian may explain further that the hypostases are distinct, but power, wisdom, and love are common divine attributes. Each divine hypostasis has (numerically) the same divine power, wisdom, and love (see Athanasius 2011: 82–83). A triad of statements is frequent in the tradition to teach something about the Trinity. But one scholastic theologian, Henry of Ghent, argued for a specific triad that bears directly on this question about the "one God" and "the Father."

According to Henry (1953: 260rR, which is *Summa* Article 72, Question 3), it is appropriate that Scripture uses the term "God" (or, the one God) to refer to the Father because of the Father's personal property of being uncaused. Moreover, Henry (like Aquinas) contends that we should appropriate divine attributes having to do with the divine intellect to the Son because the Son is also called "the Word" (John 1:1; Williams 2010); hence, the Son "is the divine wisdom" (1 Corinthians 1:24). Likewise, Henry contends that we should appropriate divine attributes having to do with the divine will to the Holy Spirit because (according to Henry) the Holy Spirit is somehow the love between the Father and the Son (see Williams 2022b; Forthcoming-a); hence, "the Holy Spirit is the divine love." While ontologically speaking the divine hypostases share numerically the same divine nature, wisdom, and love, and so are numerically the same divine nature, wisdom, and love, it may be pedagogically useful to ascribe one divine attribute to one divine hypostasis, and other divine attributes to other divine hypostases. By making a triad of statements like this, a theologian teaches others something about the Son and the Holy Spirit.

For Henry, we should appropriate to the Father the divine attributes that are explanatorily prior to the divine intellect and will, namely the divine nature and the name "God." We should appropriate the name "one God" to the Father because of the three (proposed) facts in the monarchy of the Father. There is a pragmatic reason for saying that "the Father is the one God": to teach us about the monarchy of the Father. All of this is consistent with also saying that "the Son is the one God," and "the Holy Spirit is the one God." For, the *semantics* of the statement expresses numerical predication such that it is true that the Father is divine, the Son is divine, and the Holy Spirit is divine. But the conversational *pragmatics* of saying that "the Father is the one God" is different from the semantic content of the sentence (see Korta and Perry 2019). The pragmatics gets the speaker or listener to consider the monarchy of the Father. The semantics gets the speaker or listener to consider that the Father is divine (i.e., that the one [trope of the] divine nature is predicated of the Father). If all of this is right, or at least close to the truth, then it is mistaken to suppose that "the Father is the one God" is a numerical identity statement.

## 3.3 Equality

A traditional claim is that the monarchy of the Father secures the equality between the divine hypostases. If the divine hypostases are equal, then they share all the same powers and actions (see Didymus the Blind 2011: 166–214). According to Conciliar Trinitarianism, they share *numerically the same* powers and actions. According to John of Damascus, we can ascribe "pericoheresis" to the divine hypostases (in Latin, the term is "circumincessio") (see Twombly 2015). This is a way of naming a specific mutual relation between the divine hypostases that is other than the *being generated* and *proceeding from* relations. This relation obtains between the divine hypostases as (already) constituted. Sometimes it is understood as "mutual indwelling" (see John 14:11). The upshot is that the divine hypostases share *numerically the same* divine essence, *and* the hypostases are not identical to each other because each has an unshareable personal property. This mutual relation is symmetrical and transitive. This may be the ENSWI relation with the sortal being the divine nature. If the Father is ENSWI to the Son, then (by symmetry) the Son is ENSWI to the Father. And if the Son is ENSWI to the Holy Spirit, then (by transitivity) the Father is ENSWI to the Holy Spirit.

According to a Miaphysite three-instantiation model, the divine hypostases share specifically the same powers and actions, but not numerically the same powers and actions. Specific sameness seems to secure their equality. In creaturely cases, this is precisely what happens. If two cats share merely specifically the same power to jump, and each uses their own power to jump, then they are equal in power and action. But is an equality based on specifically the same (but not numerically the same) powers and actions consistent with Conciliar Trinitarianism?

The traditional understanding of the monarchy of the Father is supposed to rule out that there are *two* (or more) divine powers (specifically the same, but numerically distinct powers). There is only one ultimate divine power, and not two (or more) ultimate divine powers of the same type. There are two reasons to suppose that a traditional understanding of the monarchy of the Father rules out two or more powers (that are specifically the same but numerically distinct). First, it is common to find arguments for the conclusion that only the Father is the cause of the Son and of the Holy Spirit (see Gregory Palamas 2022: 91–101). This is meant to deny the claim that the Father and the Son have numerically distinct powers and that they jointly cause the Holy Spirit. Second, it is common to find arguments that there is "one God" because the Father is the only cause of the Son and the Holy Spirit. If the Son were an additional cause of the Holy Spirit, then there would be two Gods. But Christians believe that there is only one God. It should be no surprise then to find that some advocates of a three-instantiation model *deny* the monarchy of the Father. There was an anonymous compiler of Miaphysite texts who affirms a "monarchy of the divine nature" (and not a monarchy of the Father) (see Ebied 2021: 125). A monarchy of the essence could mean either that all divine hypostases are specifically the same divinity, and each is uncaused, or all divine hypostases are (somehow) numerically the same divinity and each is uncaused. Contemporary philosophical theologians William Lane Craig, Keith Yandell, and R. T. Mullins deny that the Son and Holy Spirit are in any sense caused by the Father (see Hasker, 2013: 214–225; Mullins 2023). But denying that the Son and Holy Spirit are from the Father is inconsistent with Conciliar Trinitarianism (it contradicts the Nicene-Constantinople creed).

One of the worries is that saying that the Son is caused doesn't seem to fit with the prior belief that God is metaphysically necessary (see Williams Forthcoming-a). The worry might be expressed by using the language of the eleventh-century medieval Islamic philosopher Ibn Sina (Avicenna). For Ibn Sina, any essence or nature is either necessary in itself (formally necessary) or necessarily from another essence or nature (possible in itself, necessary from another) (see Ibn Sina 2007: 211–212). The former essence is identical to its own existence. The latter essence is not identical to its own existence and gets its existence from another essence. If one says that God the Son is caused, then it would seem that the Son's essence is not necessary in itself but gets its existence from the Father. But the Son's essence is not a contingent being. So the Son's essence is necessary in itself. Hence, the Son is not caused to exist by the Father.

This worry can be addressed by making further distinctions (see Henry of Ghent 2021: 241–242, which is *Summa* Article 59, Question 2, Response to Objection 1). First, we must distinguish a hypostasis and its essence or nature. Second, we must distinguish what is formally necessary, what is principiatively possible, and what is formally possible. A hypostasis who is formally necessary cannot fail to exist because its nature cannot fail to exist. A hypostasis who is principiatively possible can be the end term of a productive act. A hypostasis who is formally possible can fail to exist because its nature can fail to exist. All creatures are principiatively possible *and* formally possible. All created hypostases can be produced (created) and may or may not exist. But God the Son and God the Holy Spirit are not created hypostases. For, God the Son and God the Holy Spirit share an essence that is formally necessary (i.e., the one trope of the divine essence). But as a hypostasis, each is principiatively possible. This means that the Son and Holy Spirit are, and so can be, the end term of an internal divine productive act. God the Son's essence is formally necessary such that God the Son's hypostatic property is necessarily united in the Son with the one divine nature. The Son, in virtue of the divine essence, is formally necessary and so is not from *another* essence. And the Son in virtue of being the hypostasis that the Son is, is principiatively possible. Consequently, while the Son and Holy Spirit are each the end term of an internal divine productive act, it does not follow that the Son or Holy Spirit is a creature. Whereas all creatures are formally possible, neither the Son nor the Holy Spirit are formally possible (in the sense given).

## 3.4 The *Filioque*

The original version of the Nicene-Constantinople creed proclaims that "the Holy Spirit is the Lord and giver of life, who proceeds from the Father, and together with the Father and the Son is worshiped and glorified" (Tanner 1990: 24). But it was a later regional council, the third council of Toledo in AD 589 that added the clause "who proceeds from the Father *and the Son*" (see Percival 1988: 166; Siecienski 2010: 68–69). This was in large part a response to the adoptionist controversy, whether God the Son assumed a human nature, or adopted a human hypostasis at some point in the life of that human hypostasis. Part of the authoritative support for this addition came from texts by Augustine who affirmed the *filioque* (see Siecienski 2010: 59–66). In the eleventh council in Toledo in AD 675, the Spanish regional council argued that since the Holy Spirit is known to be the love or holiness of the Father and the Son, it follows that the Holy Spirit proceeds from the Father *and the Son* (Denzinger 1965: 176; Neuner and Dupuis 1982: 104). What is peculiar about this argument is that the premise violates a rule that Augustine made explicit in his *On the Trinity*, namely that the Holy Spirit does not do the loving for the Father or the Son (see Williams 2010: 39–40). Saying that the Holy Spirit is the love of the Father and Son is *appropriated* speech, and not one directly disclosing the ontology of the Holy Spirit's hypostatic property. If the Holy Spirit were literally the Father and Son's love, then the Holy Spirit would be a volitional act and not a hypostasis. But the Holy Spirit is a hypostasis, and so is not reducible to an act of love (see Williams 2022b).

In the late 400s or early 500s, a creed was composed in Latin, and (falsely) ascribed to Athanasius. According to this "pseudo-Athanasian" creed, the Holy Spirit "proceeds from the Father and the Son." However, if we look at the record of the first seven ecumenical councils, this clause was not added to the creed, or discussed, by any of these ecumenical councils. In every single text of the sixth ecumenical council in which there is reference to the procession of the Holy Spirit, it says that the "Holy Spirit proceeds from the Father" (see Riedinger 1990: 392–393, 418–419; 1992: 716–717, 770–771). In one place, they quote a confession of faith by Gregory Thaumaturgis, who wrote, "[the] Holy Spirit proceeds from the Father, and is clearly manifested through the Son to human beings" (Riedinger 1990: 220; see Siecienski 2010: 68). The view that the Holy Spirit eternally proceeds only from the Father, and is revealed to human beings through Jesus Christ, was endorsed by the Eastern Orthodox council of Jerusalem in AD 1672 (see Robertson 1899: 20–21).

The addition of the *filioque*-clause has been a source of significant division between the Eastern Orthodox (including other Orthodox churches) and the Roman Catholic church. There are many debates between theologians on this issue. The key concepts are that there is the eternal procession of the Holy Spirit, and there is the revelation of the Holy Spirit in and through the life of Jesus Christ. (Typically, the latter is expressed by saying that such and such a divine hypostasis is "sent" – that is, revealed to human beings.) Both parties agree to this.

On one hand, the Eastern Orthodox insist on the basis of their Scriptural exegesis and ecumenical conciliar statements that the Holy Spirit (eternally) proceeds (only) from the Father. For them, the Scriptural basis for the non-*filioque* account is John 15:26. All other Scriptural passages are interpreted as consistent with the Father, Son, and Holy Spirit's numerical unity of action. The incarnate Son's sending of the Holy Spirit at Pentecost is an act shared by all divine hypostases. The incarnate Son reveals to human beings the existence and work of the Holy Spirit. On the other hand, most Roman Catholics insist on the basis of their Scriptural exegesis and key passages from respected theologians (especially Augustine of Hippo) that the Holy Spirit (eternally) proceeds from the Father *and the Son* (see Siecienski 2010: 51–72). For them, the Son's sending the Holy Spirit at Pentecost should be interpreted as a hypostatic act by the Father and Son, but not by the Holy Spirit. This not only reveals the existence of the Holy Spirit to human beings, but also the Holy Spirit's eternal procession from the Father and Son. Protestant theologians typically side with the Roman Catholics (see Barth 2004: 473–487; Swain 2023: 214), and many mainline Protestant denominations include the *filioque* when declaring the Nicene-Constantinople creed.

What is at stake in this interpretive dispute, among other things, is where to draw the distinction between "hypostatic acts" (i.e., an act that is not common to all divine hypostases) and "common acts" (i.e., an act that is common to all divine hypostases). Is the sending of the Holy Spirit a hypostatic act (only by the Father and Son) or a common act (by the Father, Son, and Holy Spirit)? If it is an act common to all divine hypostases, then the hypostatic difference between the Son and Holy Spirit is indicated elsewhere in the New Testament. (Mark of Ephesus is emphatic that it is found in John 15:26. See Siecienski 2010: 158–159.) If it is an act by the Father and Son, but not also by the Holy Spirit, then the hypostatic difference between the Son and Holy Spirit is given, but at the cost of implying the denial of the divine hypostases sharing numerically the same action regarding creatures.

Some Roman Catholics (see Henry of Ghent 2015: 203–216) argue that the *filioque* was implicit in the original Nicene-Constantinople creed such that the addition was a clarification and not additional new content (see Siecienski 2010: 151–172). The reasoning is that in the creed, we first hear about the Father, then about the Son, and then about the Holy Spirit. Since the Son is from the Father (through being generated), and the Holy Spirit is (explanatorily) posterior to the generation of the Son, it follows that the Father and the Son are (explanatorily) prior to the Holy Spirit. Moreover, the Father's power to spirate the Holy Spirit is in the Father's divine nature. Since the Father shares this divine nature with the Son, the Son also has this power to spirate the Holy Spirit. Furthermore, the Roman Catholic view under consideration affirms that the divine hypostases share *numerically the same powers*. So, the Father and Son share numerically the same power to spirate the Holy Spirit, and so they both (eternally) exercise this power in producing the Holy Spirit. There are not two productive powers, but one productive power. Consequently, the Holy Spirit is said to "proceed from the Father and the Son." This is a philosophical argument for the *filioque*. There are other such arguments, but this is what I take to be a core philosophical argument for the *filioque*.

### A Core Philosophical Argument for the *Filioque*

P1: If (i) the Father's power to spirate the Holy Spirit is in the divine nature, (ii) the Father shares this divine nature with the Son, and (iii) the Son exists explanatorily prior to the Holy Spirit, then (iv) the Son has numerically the same power as the Father for spirating the Holy Spirit.

P2: If (iv) the Son has numerically the same power as the Father for spirating the Holy Spirit, then (v) the Father and the Son produce the Holy Spirit such that the Holy Spirit proceeds from the Father and the Son.

P3 (i)–(iii) obtain.

Therefore,

C1: (iv) obtains. [P1, P3 Modus Ponens]

Therefore,

C2: (v) obtains [P2, C1 Modus Ponens]

There are different ways that one who resists this argument might respond. For example, Gregory Palamas denies that there is a power in the divine essence for generating the Son or for spirating the Holy Spirit (Gregory Palamas 2022: 93, 95). So, he would deny P3 because he denies (i). Most Latin scholastic theologians would affirm (i) because of their metaphysical account of a power. Is a power to do $x$ a real relation to its end term? Or is a power to do $x$ an absolute thing that exists in a hypostasis, and by which a hypostasis can produce $x$? Scholastics deny that all powers are just real relations to their end term. (The view that a power is just a real relation to its end term is called the Megarian theory of power [see Lowe and Shaftoe Forthcoming; Paasch 2012: 151–163].) They deny this because it is intelligible to distinguish between one's power to do $x$, or to produce $x$, and one's exercising this power. So, if the Father spirates the Holy Spirit, then the Father *can* spirate the Holy Spirit. In virtue of what, then, is the Father able to spirate the Holy Spirit? It can't be in virtue of the relation of the Father to the Holy Spirit that the Father can spirate the Holy Spirit, because the power to produce $x$ is explanatorily prior to the exercise of this power. So, if the Father's power to spirate the Holy Spirit is not the Father's relation to the Holy Spirit, then it must be in the Father's absolute divine nature. Hence, the power to spirate is in the Father's absolute divine nature.

One response to this line of reasoning is to deny that the Father exercises any power for the Holy Spirit to proceed from the Father. It's just a relation from the Father to the Holy Spirit. However, Greek theologians affirm that the Father causes the Holy Spirit (see Gregory of Nyssa 1986: 160; Gregory of Nazianzus 2002: 71; Gregory Palamas 2022: 139–151; John of Damascus 2022: 77). If the Father's relation to the Holy Spirit is in some sense causal, then the Father surely has a causal power by which the Father causes the Holy Spirit. It seems that the Latin scholastic argument is persuasive in establishing that the Father has a power to spirate the Holy Spirit and that this power is in the divine nature. (These scholastics deny that any "actualization" from potency to actuality is required. Hence, there is no real change that occurs in the production of the Holy Spirit. Power in this sense is not contrary to act(uality) [see Aquinas 1975: 83; Paasch 2012: 122–126; Williams Forthcoming-a].)

A further response on behalf of the Greek side is this. If the power to spirate is in the divine nature and all divine hypostases share numerically the same divine nature, then all divine hypostases would exercise this power (see Gregory Palamas 2022: 97). If the Holy Spirit were to exercise this power, then the Holy Spirit would be (efficiently) caused by the Father, Son, and the Holy Spirit. But the Holy Spirit is not an (efficient) self-cause. Consequently, the Holy Spirit doesn't have the power to spirate, and in turn, this power to spirate is not in the shared divine nature. A Latin response is this: A divine hypostasis can have a power but not exercise it just in the case that another divine hypostasis (or hypostases) "already" (so to speak) exercises it. (Some assume that such a power can be exercised only "once"; others give an argument for this assumption [see Cross 2005: 148–149].) In the case of God the Son, the Son has the power to generate the Son, but the Son doesn't exercise this power because the Father "already" exercises it, and it is logically contradictory for the Son to be an (efficient) self-cause. Likewise, the Holy Spirit has the power to spirate himself, but doesn't exercise this power for the same reason that the Son doesn't exercise the power to generate the Son.

Another response to the *Core Philosophical Argument for the Filioque* would be to deny P3 by denying that (iii) there is any order between the generation of the Son and the procession of the Holy Spirit. If there is no order between the generation of the Son and the procession of the Holy Spirit, then the Son does not exist explanatorily prior to the Holy Spirit. If the Son does not exist explanatorily prior to the Holy Spirit, then the Son and Holy Spirit are explanatorily simultaneous with each other. If the Father generates the Son and spirates the Holy Spirit at the same explanatory instant, then the Son would have the power to spirate the Holy Spirit, but the Father "already" exercises it. Consequently, the Holy Spirit would not proceed from the Father *and the Son*, but only from the Father.

What philosophical reasons, then, are there for supposing that there is an order between the generation of the Son and the procession of the Holy Spirit? If we don't have any plausible reasons for positing such an order, then we might as well consider conceding that the Holy Spirit proceeds only from the Father. One rationale starts from opposed relations and infers to the ordered exercise of different powers. Anselm of Canterbury and Thomas Aquinas argued that there must be something that distinguishes the Son and the Holy Spirit. What distinguishes them is not some real absolute entity, but rather personal relations. After all, it is traditional to claim that the divine hypostases are distinct only by personal relations – that their "idiomata" are real relations. Suppose this were true. According to Aquinas, the only kind of relation that would distinguish divine hypostases are opposed relations. That is, opposed relations are a pair of relations, one of which is a principle of another, and the other is what or who is from that principle (roughly, cause and effect are opposed relations) (see

Aquinas 1945: 344–348, which is *Summa Theologiae* Part 1, Article 36, Question 2). Opposed relations are irreflexive, asymmetrical, and simultaneous. So, for example, the first divine hypostasis is the "Father of the Son," and the second divine hypostasis is the "Son of the Father." (The Father isn't the Father of himself, nor is the Son the Son of himself.) But the Holy Spirit cannot be distinct by a relation opposed only to the Father; for then the Holy Spirit would have an identical relation that the Son has to the Father. In which case, the Son and Holy Spirit would not be distinct hypostases. But they are distinct hypostases. So, the Holy Spirit must have an opposed relation to the Father *and the Son*. Thus, the Holy Spirit would be Spirit of the Father and the Son, and they would be one spirator of the Holy Spirit (see Tanner 1990: 526–527; Siecienski 2010: 151–172). For these reasons, the Father generates the Son, the Son has the power to spirate, and (explanatorily posterior) the Father and Son jointly spirate the Holy Spirit (see Aquinas 1975: 93). (Interestingly, Aquinas admits that it's philosophically possible that the Holy Spirit is from the Father, and the Son is from the Father and the Holy Spirit. But, he says, "nobody says that"; see Aquinas [1945: 345, which is *Summa Theologiae* Part 1, Article 36, Question 2].)

A different rationale has been put forward for asserting that there must be an order between the generation of the Son and the procession of the Holy Spirit. Advocates of this account include Henry of Ghent and Duns Scotus. In this proposal, there is an order between the Son and Holy Spirit because the Son is generated from the exercise of an *intellectual* power in the one divine nature and the Holy Spirit proceeds from the exercise of a *volitional* power in the one divine nature (see Cross 2005: 132–142). If we assume that any act of will requires a prior act of intellect, then we would say that an intellectual productive action is prior to a volitional productive action. Hence, if the Son is the end term of an intellectual productive action and the Holy Spirit is the end term of a volitional productive action, then the Son's being generated is prior to the Holy Spirit's procession. Consequently, there is an order from the Father, to the Son, and to the Holy Spirit. The Father intellectually generates the Son, and so communicates the one divine nature to the Son. Next in the explanatory order is the fact that the Father *and the Son* have numerically the same volitional productive power for spirating the Holy Spirit. Since they both have numerically the same volitional productive power, it follows that they volitionally spirate the Holy Spirit. They are not two causes but one cause of the Holy Spirit. Thus, the Holy Spirit proceeds from the Father and the Son (see Friedman 2007: 124–148; 2010: 66–68; Williams Forthcoming-a).

These are two accounts that each explain why there is an order between the generation of the Son and the procession of the Holy Spirit. There are two ways that the Greek side of the debate responds. The first approach denies that the argument is sound by denying that the *filioque* is true on the basis of Scriptural exegesis and the authority of the Nicene-Constantinople creed. The second approach finds fault with each account and proposes an alternative account.

Greek theologians agree that the Father is the cause of the Son and the cause of the Holy Spirit. But they deny that the Son is a co-cause of the Holy Spirit. What distinguishes the Son and the Holy Spirit is not based on the number of divine hypostases from whom they are (*contra* the opposed-relations account), but *how* they are from the Father. As the Nicene-Constantinople creed says, the Son is *generated* by the Father, and the Holy Spirit *proceeds* from the Father. Generation and procession are different ways that the Son and Holy Spirit are caused by the Father (see Gregory of Nyssa 1986: 160; Gregory Nazianzus 2002: 122–123). This reply challenges the plausibility of the opposed-relations account on the grounds that the opposed relations do not give a plausible explanation of the nonidentity between divine hypostases as expressed in the Nicene-Constantinople creed. If it did, then we should find the language or concepts of opposed relations. But such is not explicit. Instead, we find language about different *ways* that the Son and Holy Spirit are from the Father, namely by generation and procession.

Moreover, the Greek side challenges the second explanation that appeals to diverse powers in the one divine nature, namely an intellectual productive power and a volitional productive power. While the creed speaks of generation, it does not speak of *intellectual* generation; and while the creed speaks of procession, it does not speak of *volitional* procession. Despite this response to the diverse-powers account (sometimes labeled the psychological account), some Greek theologians, including Gregory of Nyssa, do sometimes use a psychological analogy. This raises the question: What's the pedagogical point of giving a psychological analogy? Is it to explain the actual ways in which the Son and Holy Spirit are related to the Father? Or is it a starting point in a longer educational conversation for pointing toward there being numerically the same divine essence or nature in the Father, Son, and Holy Spirit (see Maspero 2023b: 202–229)? It seems to me that the latter is the case. They are not given as models (accounts) of the Trinity, but they are more limited in getting someone to conceive of how there can be three hypostases with numerically the same divine nature.

But there is a positive development that can be made for the Greek side in relation to the diverse-powers account. The Latin side contends that the Father exercises a power for the generation of the Son, and a different power for the procession of the Holy Spirit. The Greek side should deny that these powers are intellectual and volitional, and stick with generative power and processive power. If this were conceded, then it can be said that the Father exercises each of these powers at the same explanatory instant. This would rule out there being an *order* between the Father's exercise of these two internal divine productive powers. For, while the Son would have the processive power, the Father would "already" have exercised it, such that the Son would be "too late" to exercise it with the Father. Hence, the Greek side can concede to the Latin side that the Father (eternally) exercises two different powers in the divine essence, but this does not imply the *filioque* and is in fact incompatible with the *filioque*. The upshot for the Greek side is that it undermines the *Core Philosophical Argument* for the *filioque*, *and* advances the Greek side. This is a mediating position between the Greek side and the Latin side, and it is worth considering.

Is the *filioque* consistent with Conciliar Trinitarianism? If the Latins are right that it is implicit in the Nicene-Constantinople creed, then it is consistent with Conciliar Trinitarianism. What philosophically supports the claim that the *filioque* should be made explicit in the creed is the *Core Philosophical Argument*. But, if the Greeks are right that the negation of the *filioque* is implicit in the Nicene-Constantinople creed, then it would be inconsistent with Conciliar Trinitarianism. Gregory Palamas, for example, argues that just as the Son is the "*only*-begotten" of the Father, so too is it implied that the Holy Spirit proceeds *only* from the Father (see Gregory Palamas 2022: 79–85). He claims that the second "only" (by parallelism) is implied by the first "only" that applies to the Son. It seems that philosophy alone cannot settle this dispute about whether the *filioque* is implicit in the Nicene-Constantinople creed from AD 381. The Latins have their arguments and their exegesis of Scripture for the *filioque*, and the Greeks have their arguments and their exegesis of Scripture against the *filioque*. The dispute is not merely linguistic, or political. It is a substantive theological, philosophical, and exegetical disagreement.

## 3.5 The Debate and Dilemmas about Real Relations

According to Conciliar Trinitarianism, the Father eternally causes the Son, and the Father eternally causes the Holy Spirit. These two claims are together called "internal divine production." These productions are not contingent, nor is the relevant productive power a potency that is contrary to actuality; instead, the productive action is always and necessarily united to the productive power. There is no time at which there isn't the Son or Holy Spirit, nor does the first divine hypostasis become the Father through a change. But given internal divine production, different accounts of what distinguishes the divine hypostases face some dilemmas. The dilemmas arise regarding the explanatory order between the divine hypostases in the context of these internal divine productions. In scholastic theology, this explanatory order was hotly debated. Although the debate I am considering here was between Latin-speaking theologians in the late thirteenth century, the explanatory order proposed bears directly on what others might say.

Consider the following three theories of the *explanatory order* (see Friedman 2010: 5–49). Thomas Aquinas contended that the first divine hypostasis is the Father because of the opposed relation to the Son. Opposed relations are simultaneous such that one is not explanatorily prior to the other. As Aquinas points out, a productive action requires an agent. The first divine hypostasis, the Father, is the agent who (eternally) generates the Son. But note that if the first hypostasis is the Father explanatorily prior to the generative action and opposed relations are simultaneous, then the Son exists explanatorily prior to the generative action. But, the generative action is supposed to explain why there is a divine hypostasis who is the Son. So, Aquinas's opposed-relations account faces a dilemma:

### A Dilemma for Opposed Relations

1. Either the first hypostasis is the Father explanatorily prior to the generation of the Son, or posterior to the generation of the Son.
2. If the first hypostasis is the Father explanatorily prior to the generation of the Son, then there is no explanatory need for the generative action because the Father-Son opposed relations are simultaneous.
3. If the first hypostasis is the Father explanatorily posterior to the generation of the Son, then there is no agent who generates the Son.

Therefore,

4. Either there is no explanatory need for the generative action because the Father-Son opposed relations are simultaneous, or there is no agent who generates the Son.

Another theory, proposed by Bonaventure, differs from the opposed-relations theory. Bonaventure affirms that the "Father of" relation and the "Son of" relation are explanatorily *posterior* to the first divine hypostasis's generative action. However, the first hypostasis is constituted in being the ungenerated (uncaused) divine hypostasis explanatorily prior to the generative action. The opposed relations that obtain between the first and second hypostases are explanatorily consequent to the generative action. (Sijuwade 2021 advocates for this proposal, though without reference to Bonaventure.) The second hypostasis is constituted as the hypostasis it is by *being generated*. This is a way of being, which is labeled a *disparate relation*. Consequent to the second hypostasis being generated, the first hypostasis is the Father of the Son, and the second hypostasis is the Son of the Father. A dilemma for this theory arises from considering the Conciliar understanding that the first hypostasis is essentially ordered to the second divine hypostasis. This is expressed by the claim that the first hypostasis is the Father of the Son. So, Bonaventure's disparate relations account faces a dilemma.

### A Dilemma for Disparate Relations

1. Either the first hypostasis is ordered to the second hypostasis explanatorily prior to the generative action, or posterior to the generative action.
2. If the first hypostasis is ordered to the second hypostasis explanatorily prior to the generative action, then the first hypostasis is not merely constituted as this hypostasis in being uncaused.
3. If the first hypostasis is ordered to the second hypostasis only explanatorily posterior to the generative action, then the first hypostasis is not constitutively ordered to the second hypostasis.
Therefore,
4. Either the first hypostasis is not merely constituted as this hypostasis in being uncaused, or the first hypostasis is not constitutively ordered to the second hypostasis.

A third theory, proposed by Henry of Ghent, attempts to fix the unacceptable implications of Aquinas's and Bonaventure's different theories. Henry claims that the first hypostasis is constituted as the first hypostasis in being generative (meaning: "will generate" in the sense of explanatory order, not temporal sequence) and who is uncaused. (This is different from generative *action*. Henry's explanatory order for the first divine hypostasis is: (i) being generative, (ii) being ungenerated, (iii) having the opportunity to generate, (iv) generating, and (v) Father [see Henry of Ghent 2021: 202; Williams Forthcoming-a].) Explanatorily posterior to being constituted, this hypostasis generates another divine hypostasis. This other hypostasis is constituted in being *generated*. The opposed relations, "Father of" and "Son of," are explanatorily posterior to the second hypostasis being constituted. Henry accepts premise 2 in the *Dilemma for Disparate Relations* and names the first hypostasis as *being generative* so that this hypostasis is constitutively ordered toward the act of generating the second hypostasis. Like Bonaventure's account, Henry's proposal is of disparate relations that are explanatorily prior to the opposed relations. For example, the second hypostasis is constituted in *being generated*, and consequently is the Son of (which is an opposed relation) the first hypostasis.

There is, however, a dilemma facing Henry's proposal. If something is a real relation, then we can identify the end term of the relation. To what, or to whom, is the relation directed? If the first hypostasis is constituted in being generative, and this is a real relation, then what (or who) is the end term of this relation?

### A Dilemma for the Generative Relation

1. Either the first hypostasis's generative relation has a real end term, or not.
2. If the first hypostasis's generative relation has a real end term, then there is someone real who is the end term of the generative relation and who is real explanatorily prior to the generative action.
3. If the first hypostasis's generative relation does not have a real end term, then the generative relation is not a real relation.

Therefore,

4. Either there is someone real that is the end term of the generative relation and who is explanatorily prior to the generative action, or the generative relation is not a real relation.

Henry's response to this dilemma brings out his theory of real relations, which is different from Aquinas's and particularly Giles of Rome's theories. Whereas Aquinas and Giles maintain that a real relation takes its reality from its end term, Henry denies this. (This is why Aquinas asserts that the Father is the Father only because of the Son; the Son is the end term of the Father's real relation.) For Henry, a real relation is real because it is founded on a real (nonrelative) foundation (see Williams 2012: 115–127). The being generative relation is founded on a real divine power, namely the power for generating (which is in the divine nature). So, the first hypostasis's relation of being generative is real because it is founded on a real power in the divine nature.

All these theories assume that what constitutes and distinguishes the divine hypostases are real relations. The disagreement is about the *species* of these real relations. It is important to note that each of these theories includes opposed relations (see Tanner 1990: 570–571). Where they differ is whether opposed relations are constitutive of the divine hypostases, or only explanatorily posterior to the divine hypostases's constitution. Lastly, it should be noted that Conciliar Trinitarianism itself does not commit to any one explanation of these real relations.

## 4 Unity of Action

### 4.1 Unity of Action in a Three-Instantiation Model

One commonly accepted claim in Trinitarian theology is that the divine hypostases's actions toward creatures are "inseparable" (see Jamieson and Wittman 2022: 106–125). The basic idea is that the divine hypostases are perfect in wisdom, power, and goodness. They always agree on what they do. This is a mark of perfect wisdom, power, and goodness. As with other areas in Trinitarian theology, the Cappodocian Fathers are a key source for thinking about the divine hypostases's "inseparable actions." As might be expected, philosophers have interpreted these statements differently.

According to those who advocate for something like the Miaphysite three-instantiation model of the Trinity, they explain the divine hypostases "inseparable actions" in terms of agreement in thought and action regarding creatures. On this model, each divine hypostasis has their own (e.g., tropes of) intellectual and volitional powers, and their own (e.g., tropes of) actions that derive from these different powers. Richard Swinburne, for example, contends that since the Father is the source of the Son and the Holy Spirit, it follows that the Son and the Holy Spirit should (and would) defer to what the Father chooses regarding the production of contingent beings, or with regard to how to respond to contingent beings (see Swinburne 1994: 172–176). The Son and the Holy Spirit would follow a moral principle according to which one should defer to the wishes of one's parent(s). According to Swinburne, the Father delegates certain spheres of activity to the Son and to the Holy Spirit. So, the Son makes the decisions with regard to some places or topics, and the others concede to what the Son chooses with regard to these places or topics. Similarly, the Father makes the decisions for other places or topics, and the others concede to what the Father chooses in these places or topics. The same holds for the Holy Spirit. This makes explicit that Swinburne contends that agreement between the divine hypostases entails that they have specifically, but not numerically, the same (e.g., tropes of) volitions.

Is Swinburne's account consistent with Conciliar Trinitarianism? It is not. Swinburne contends that the divine hypostases share specifically, but not numerically the same powers and operations (e.g., acts of intellect and acts of will). But Constantinople III is explicit that the divine hypostases not only share numerically the same powers, but also numerically the same operations (e.g., acts of intellect, acts of will). In the words of Gregory of Nyssa, it is the fact that the divine hypostases share *numerically the same nature* and powers and operations that secures the divine monarchy. Those who deny this numerical unity might propose a multitude of powers, which Gregory would call a "multitude of gods" (Gregory of Nyssa 2019: 69).

However, Swinburne addresses this worry by the supposition that the divine hypostases in fact *always* agree with each other. If they always agree with each other, then there would not be disagreement or conflict between them. However, a worry for this response arises from the plausibility of Swinburne's appeal to the moral principle that one should defer to one's parents or one's causal source (see Williams 2017: 340–342). Consider a different moral principle: A parent should defer to their child's wishes in some circumstances. In the case of the Trinity, God the Son is perfect in wisdom, power, and goodness. So, why shouldn't the Father be morally required to defer to what the Son wishes, or to what the Holy Spirit wishes? There are two competing moral principles here, and each is plausible in relevant contexts. In the case of the Trinity, though, it isn't obvious which moral principle should apply. Swinburne assumes that whatever the moral truths are, the divine hypostases do not wish or will what is immoral. Nevertheless, there are nonmoral contingent facts. Swinburne gives the example of which way that Earth revolves around the Sun. Suppose the Father chooses to create a universe in which the Earth goes one way, but the Son chooses to create a universe in which the same Earth goes the opposite way. Which moral principle should settle the disagreement? It isn't obvious (enough) which it should be. William Hasker defends Swinburne against these objections by appealing to the divine hypostases's perfect wisdom: Surely, they would come to some agreement? But, if they have a libertarian kind of free will that entails the principle of alternative possibilities (as Hasker 2013: 208–209 accepts; see Williams 2017: 342 ff.), and these are contingent nonmoral facts under consideration, then it is difficult to say what should be chosen if the agents are perfect in wisdom, goodness, and power. What is clear, however, is that this sort of account of the divine hypostases's unity of action contradicts what Gregory of Nyssa and Constantinople III say about it (see Williams 2020a: 100–101).

## 4.2 Unity of Action in a Neo-Sabellian Model

Brian Leftow has argued against what he labels "Social models" of the Trinity, in contrast to a Latin model that he endorses (see Leftow 2004a: 203–249). These Social models are much like what I've called a three-instantiation model of the divine nature. They suppose that there is a sense in which the divine nature is generic, and the hypostases are different instantiations of it (or there are three tropes of the divine nature, etc.). Leftow made popular in contemporary discourse two labels for different families of models of the Trinity: Social models and Latin models (see Williams 2013: 75–78; 2022a: 333, 356–357 for problems with Leftow's labels). This Latin model has it that there is just one trope of the divine nature. The name for this trope of the divine nature is "God." According to Leftow's Latin model, God is eternally and necessarily the subject of three simultaneous conscious lives (2007). God lives a stream of conscious thought and volition that is God the Father's life. But God also lives another stream of conscious thought and volition that is God the Son's life. And God lives a third stream of conscious thought and volition that is God the Holy Spirit's life. Since there is just the one trope of the divine nature, there is just one divine intellectual power and one divine will power. Leftow's account is influenced by specific Latin authors, that is, Boethius, Anselm, and Aquinas. Since

Boethius (unlike all the Byzantine, Syriac, and other Latin Christian theologians before and during his time [see Williams 2020b: 80–108]) includes rationality in his definition of person, Leftow supposes – going beyond Boethius and joining with John Locke – that rational acts (e.g., acts of intellect, acts of will) are directly related to what makes an entity a person. So, God the Father is a person because he is a stream of certain conscious acts (acts of intellect, acts of will). Likewise, the same holds for God the Son and God the Holy Spirit. This means that although there is one divine intellectual power and one divine will power (God's powers), God has three different streams of intellectual and volitional acts.

Suppose God the Father judges that <It would be good to create 150,000,000 puppies>. But, if this particular act of intellect is God the Father's, then it is not God the Son's nor God the Holy Spirit's. It is an open question whether God the Father's judgment of this proposition entails (guarantees) that the other divine persons also share the same judgment of the same proposition. Note that if this model implies that God the Son and God the Holy Spirit would also make specifically the same judgment but by numerically different mental acts (none are shared in the same conscious stream), then this model does not thereby have an account for why all divine persons must share the same judgment in all possible worlds.

Consider God the Father's volition to create 150,000,000 puppies. In this model, it can be that only God the Father creates 150,000,000 puppies. There is nothing that necessitates that God the Son or God the Holy Spirit also make the same judgment and will to create the same number of puppies. God could choose to create something only in one of God's conscious lives, or two of God's conscious lives, or all three of God's conscious lives. Consequently, Leftow's neo-Sabellian model of the Trinity fairs no better than other Social models of the Trinity with regard to the divine hypostases's inseparable actions.

This neo-Sabellian model faces other objections from Conciliar Trinitarianism. First, according to Constantinople III, the divine hypostases share numerically the same power and will, and also numerically the same operations. As the council reasons, if we say that there are personal wills and volitions, then in the Trinity there would be three will powers and three volitions (operations). But that is "profane" and violates "canonical logic." This neo-Sabellian model affirms the numerical unity of the divine persons' powers but denies the numerical unity of their operations. For in this model, the divine persons are distinct only if they do *not* share numerically the same (conscious) operations.

A second objection from Conciliar Trinitarianism is based on the number of divine hypostases. In this neo-Sabellian model, there is just one divine subject, God. God is three nonidentical streams of conscious acts. But, according to

Constantinople III, there is "not a hypostasis of three names, but one essence of three hypostases." This neo-Sabellian model treats God as the name of a substance or subject who is three nonidentical streams of conscious acts. It is one subject of "three names." This seems to be (nearly) equivalent to the claim that God is one hypostasis who is three nonidentical streams of conscious acts. But the Conciliar model affirms that there are three hypostases who share the one (trope of the) divine nature, and denies that there is one hypostasis that is the Father, Son, and Holy Spirit. Leftow seeks to avoid classic Sabellianism according to which God is *contingently* the Father, Son, and Holy Spirit, by means of affirming God's being eternally and necessarily the Father, Son, and Holy Spirit (Leftow 2007: 374). But Constantinople III makes clear that the root problem is in affirming just one hypostasis of three names whether contingent *or* necessary.

## 4.3 Unity of Action in a Conciliar Model

According to Constantinople III, the divine hypostases share numerically the same divine nature, powers, will, and actions. (For discussion of Gregory of Nyssa and Gregory of Nazianzus, see Holmes 2012.) This means that if, for example, the Father wills to create some puppies, then the Son and the Holy Spirit also create the same puppies. The consequent follows from the antecedent because the antecedent assumes that divine hypostases share numerically the same powers and actions that are from those powers. It is often said that the divine hypostases's actions are inseparable; this is so because their actions are *numerically* the same. (For more on numerical unity of volitional action, see Williams 2017: 333–336; 2022a: 341.)

One caveat is this. In Section 3.4, I suggested that the non-*filioque* position could philosophically bolster its position if it were admitted that there is a power for generating and a power for spirating in the one divine nature. Moreover, it would be bolstered if it admitted that neither the Son nor the Holy Spirit could exercise these two powers because these powers are "already" exercised by the Father. Suppose all this were admitted. Does this violate Constantinople III's claim that the divine hypostases share numerically the same operations? Is the act of generating an operation? Is the act of spirating an operation? Moreover, if we admit that there are some operations that cannot be shared by the divine hypostases, then why couldn't Leftow assert that it is like this in his neo-Sabellian model. Leftow could say that it's just impossible for God the Son to have *numerically the same* acts of intellect and acts of will as God the Father (even if "God" is both nonoverlapping streams of conscious acts).

There is a way to indicate how this revision to the non-*filioque* position is consistent with a Conciliar model of the Trinity. One must distinguish an internal divine production of a divine hypostasis, and actions that are not such an internal divine production. Conciliar Trinitarianism is clear that only the Father generates (produces) the Son, and (only) the Father spirates (produces) the Holy Spirit. All other actions are shared by the divine hypostases. Moreover, the Conciliar model entails that the divine hypostases share every action that is possible for them to share. (If they do share such actions, then it is possible for them to share such actions.) Since it is impossible for the Son and the Holy Spirit to produce themselves, it follows that they do not share these productive actions with the Father. For, no one is an efficient cause of their own existence.

Still, there is a worry about saying that the divine hypostases share numerically the same actions, even setting aside the Father's generation of the Son and procession of the Holy Spirit. Contemporary philosophers raise an informative objection against the claim that the divine hypostases share *numerically the same* actions. One of the most significant arguments for the claim that the divine hypostases do not share numerically the same operations (whether it's a Social model, or Leftow's neo-Sabellian model) is based on what philosophers call *de se* knowledge (see Mosser 2009; Williams 2017: 327–339). Consider the following: Mary knows that <I am Jesus's Mother>. This is a first-person kind of knowledge. It is knowledge about herself. Others know that Mary is Jesus's Mother, and John knows that <you are Jesus's Mother>, but only Mary can know that <*I* am Jesus's Mother>. *De se* knowledge is *self*-knowledge. A question for a Conciliar model of the Trinity is this: Do any of the divine hypostases have self-knowledge? If the Father has self-knowledge, then the Father and only the Father would know that <*I* am God the Father>. The Son could know different propositions, like <*I* am not God the Father> and <God the Father is God the Father>. If we were to ascribe to God the Son knowledge that <*I* am God the Father>, then that would seem to suggest that God the Son has a false belief (or something like a false belief). But God the Son doesn't have any false beliefs because God the Son is omniscient. If an advocate of a Conciliar model of the Trinity accepted that each divine hypostasis has self-knowledge, then it would seem that there are (putative) cases in which the divine hypostases do *not* share numerically the same operations, particularly intellectual acts of self-knowledge. So, a pro-Conciliar model needs to address this objection. Section 5.3 does that.

## 5 The Problem of Self-Knowledge in the Trinity

Conciliar Trinitarianism says that there are three divine hypostases, and just one shared (trope of the) divine being ("ousia"), nature ("phusis"), power ("dunamis"), and so on. Now consider another claim: The divine *hypostases* are omniscient. They are omniscient because of their (shared) divine nature. The divine nature includes the divine attribute of omniscience. There are not three instances of divine omniscience (one for each divine hypostasis), but rather just one case of divine omniscience. So, now consider this question: Does the Father know which divine hypostasis they (sg.) are? ("They" is used as a singular pronoun here. Consider this example: "does that student over there know that they are late to class?") Does the Son know which divine hypostasis they are? Does the Holy Spirit know which divine hypostasis they are? Surely, if a hypostasis is omniscient, then that hypostasis knows which hypostasis they (sg.) are?

## 5.1 An Apophatic Response: Fundamental Truths and Nonfundamental Truths

Theologians have responded in different ways to claims about what is intrinsic to the Trinity. One strain of Christian theology is apophatic (in Latin, it's called the *via negativa* [way of negation]). In general, apophaticism is deeply impressed with divine transcendence over all creatures. The divine nature and divine hypostases in themselves are ineffable, inconceivable, and incomprehensible. Given such divine transcendence, not only should we be extremely cautious in what we say about the Trinity, we should suppose that we do not have access to the fundamental truths concerning the Trinity, but only nonfundamental truths (see Jacobs 2015). A fundamental truth is how things are in reality; a nonfundamental truth is a truth that is made true by some fundamental truth. Suppose that in reality there are no tables, but there are particles arranged table-wise. If one points and asserts "that is a table," what they say is literally true. But the reality that makes the statement true is not a table, but particles arranged table-wise. Jacobs (2015: 67) contends that fundamental truths concerning the Trinity are ineffable. That is, there are fundamental truths, but there are no fundamental true *propositions* concerning the Trinity because fundamental truths can't be represented by propositions. Nevertheless, there are nonfundamental true propositions that are effable.

If Jacobs is right, then any true statement concerning the Trinity in this Element would be a nonfundamental truth and not a fundamental truth. There's something real that makes these nonfundamental propositions true, but there is no fundamental proposition that can express this reality at its joints. An implication of this account of apophaticism is that it is consistent with saying that each divine hypostasis has, or does not have, *de se* knowledge. Whatever truth is expressed by the relevant proposition, it would be a nonfundamental truth.

However, one may worry whether this apophaticism is committed to anti-realism concerning the Trinity (see Jacobs 2015: 169–171). For, if Conciliar

Trinitarianism is true, then what distinguishes the divine hypostases must *be* certain fundamental nonidentical items (e.g., real relations). Moreover, even if creatures cannot *perfectly* express by way of a proposition the distinctions between the divine hypostases, surely, the divine hypostases do so (being omniscient). Hence, there are fundamental nonidentical items that make true (our imperfect) propositions regarding the Trinity. Moreover, Jacobs appeals to Brower's account of divine simplicity to defend his position. But whereas Brower's "truthmaker" account of divine simplicity does *not* pertain to the Trinity, Jacobs extends it to the Trinity. Brower does not apply this account of simplicity to the Trinity but only to the divine essence; he has argued for a *constitution* model of the Trinity (see Section 2.3). For, there are coherence problems if one applies this account of simplicity to the Trinity (see Section 6.2). Consequently, Jacobs's account needs revision in light of coherence worries regarding simplicity and the Trinity (see Williams Forthcoming-b for more discussions).

## 5.2 Non-Conciliar, Affirmative Responses

Another kind of response is to affirm that each divine hypostasis knows which divine hypostasis they (sg.) are, and this is explained by appeal to some version of the three-instantiation model of the Trinity. William Hasker has articulated an updated version of the three-instantiation model of the divine nature. According to Hasker, there is no abstract divine nature that is instantiated once for each divine hypostasis. Instead, the divine nature is concrete, and it constitutes the three divine hypostases. (This constitution relation is asymmetrical.) But, like the older three-instantiation model of the divine nature, Hasker distinguishes between a divine hypostasis being fully divine *and* being like a part in relation to the whole divine nature (Hasker 2013: 249). Hasker agrees with the Pseudo-Athanasian creed that we should not *say* that there are three eternals and three almighty beings, but he nevertheless believes that there *are* three eternals and three almighty beings (Hasker 2013: 249–254). The older version is that there is a generic divine nature that is instantiated by each hypostasis, and that each hypostasis is like a part of the whole divine nature.

Hasker's proposal is an improvement over the older version to the extent that it is consistent with the Conciliar claim that the divine nature only exists in divine hypostases, and so is not an abstract nature but a concrete nature. Nevertheless, it retains other logical inconsistencies that the older version has in relation to Conciliar Trinitarianism. For Hasker, the divine hypostases are "distinct centers of consciousness" such that they do not share any numerically the same (mental) acts. Given this, Hasker affirms that each divine hypostasis has *de se* knowledge by means of an unshared (and unshareable) mental act. While this model is internally coherent, it is inconsistent with the Conciliar Trinitarian claim that the divine hypostases share *numerically the same powers and acts/operations*.

Leftow's Neo-Sabellian model gives a different account (2004b: 326–328). Whereas Hasker gives an account according to which a divine hypostasis has a mental act directed at themselves, Leftow's ultimate subject is God, and not a divine hypostasis (e.g., God the Father) like Hasker has it. So, Leftow rejects the theory according to which "I" has pure reference by virtue of the subject using the term "I." For, in Leftow's telling, God is the subject using the "I" *in a certain conscious life stream*. So, Leftow proposes that self-knowledge that includes a use of "I" requires a mode of presentation. This means that God the Father would think a proposition like <I, in my Fatherly stream of conscious life, am God the Father>. It cannot simply be the subject (i.e., God) that contributes the reference of the term "I." If that were the case, then God in his Fatherly stream of conscious life would believe (falsely) that <I, in my Fatherly stream of conscious life, am God the Holy Spirit>. Instead, Leftow says that God can reference God's other conscious life streams, such that in God's Fatherly conscious life stream, God can know that <I, in my Holy Spirit life stream, am God the Holy Spirit>. In this account, self-knowledge in the Trinity requires a certain mode of presentation – adding "in my X conscious life" – rather than the more standard account according to which the subject is sufficient in contributing to the reference of a use of "I."

This account is inconsistent with Conciliar Trinitarianism because it denies that the divine hypostases share numerically the same acts or operations, here, conscious mental acts. Although Leftow's model implies that numerically the same God has all of these mental acts such that there is no divine mental act that God doesn't have, nevertheless, God-as-Father shares no mental act that God-as-Son has. None of God's conscious life streams overlap each other (or are a part of each other).

## 5.3 Two Conciliar Responses: A Conciliar Non-Social Model and a Conciliar Social Model

The philosopher John Perry (1993) introduced his theory of the pure reference of the essential indexical "I" according to which the one using the term "I" is sufficient in contributing to the reference of "I." Perry gives an illustration. Suppose that you are pushing your grocery cart through a grocery store. You notice a line of sugar on the aisle floor, and you think that somebody has a bag of sugar in their grocery cart that is spilling onto the aisle. But then you make a turn around the corner and discover that "*I* am the one with the sugar spilling onto the floor!" Perry introduces this to illustrate that the indexical term "I" gets its reference from the one who is using it. This is the beginning of a plausible theory about how the term "I" has its reference. But now consider this: Perry's example begins with a fact about a bag of sugar spilling on a floor, and ends with a slightly different fact, namely a person in relation to a bag of sugar spilling on the floor. The realization that "It was my bag of sugar!" adds a metaphysical relation of a person to a bag of sugar that is spilling on the floor. Now suppose somebody else, Juan, also noticed that a bag of sugar was spilling onto the aisle floor. And suppose that Juan witnessed you realize that it was your bag of sugar spilling on the floor. Both of you know the same facts: You both know that a bag of sugar was spilling on the floor, and that it was your bag of sugar spilling on the aisle floor. The question arises: In this story, is there some fact that you know that Juan does not know? It seems plausible that you know the same facts. This response is analogous to a B-theorist about time who says that A-facts (temporal indexical facts: pastness, presentness, and futureness) are reducible to B-facts (nonindexical facts: at earlier time t1, at simultaneous time t2, and at later time t3) (see Koons and Pickavance 2015: 182–185). If this is plausible, then one might apply this to the question about self-knowledge in the Trinity.

This response *denies* first-personal knowledge. Call this a Conciliar *non-Social* model. (I develop this account further in Williams Forthcoming-b.) This account reduces facts of a first-person perspective to facts of a third-person perspective. What motivates this denial is the thought that self-knowledge is not really different from third-personal knowledge. The same fact can be known in different ways. Peter knows that <I am Peter>, but Paul can also know that <Peter is Peter>. Note that a way to disambiguate <I am Peter> could be to insert the name Peter in the subject position so that it is <I, Peter, am Peter>. If that is plausible, then it can be reduced to the fact that <Peter is Peter>. There would be no need to posit any divine hypostasis using "I" for self-knowledge.

In this Conciliar non-Social model, God the Father has a mental act with the propositional content <The Father is the Father>, and likewise God the Son and God the Holy Spirit share numerically the same mental act such that all divine hypostases know that <The Father is the Father>. If a use of the indexical term "I" does not give one cognitive access to a fact that couldn't also be accessed through a third-personal proposition, then we have a response to the question about self-knowledge in the Trinity. That is, there is self-knowledge in the sense that, for example, God the Father knows that <God the Father is the Father>, and so too do the other divine hypostases. But no indexical terms are required for this knowledge. This proposal is consistent with Conciliar Trinitarianism because the divine hypostases share all the same mental acts, including third-personal acts that approximate self-knowledge.

But if there is a difference between first-personal self-knowledge that requires a use of "I" and third-personal self-knowledge that does not require any use of "I," and we have reason to suppose that there is first-personal self-knowledge in the Trinity, then we would need a different response to show how Conciliar Trinitarianism can be consistent with such first-personal self-knowledge. This would be a Conciliar *Social* model of the Trinity (see Williams 2017; 2020a; 2021).

In this Conciliar Social model, an intellectual act with propositional content has an explanation for why it has the content it has (as opposed to assuming that it is a brute fact). Suppose that just as there are spoken sentences and written sentences with semantic and syntactic content, so too are there mental sentences with semantic and syntactic content. Further, we need to distinguish sentence-types and sentence-tokens. A sentence-type is a sentence that can be instantiated multiple times. A sentence-token is one occurrence or trope of a sentence-type; it is not multiply-instantiable. Further, like some sentence-types, some sentence-tokens consist of something in the subject position, a verb, and something in the predicate position. If the verb is the copula ("is"), then it can be used to express different relations. Candidate relations include specific predication, numerical identity, other identity relations (e.g., Beall's *subclassical* identity), numerical sameness without identity, and numerical predication. Moreover, it is possible that numerically the same sentence-token is used in a context to express different propositions. For example, consider an interaction between Bilbo Baggins and Gandalf the Grey in Tolkien's *The Hobbit*:

> "Good Morning!" said Bilbo, and he meant it. The sun was shining, and the grass was very green. But Gandalf looked at him from under long bushy eyebrows that stuck out further than the brim of his shady hat. "What do you mean?" he said. "Do you wish me a good morning, or mean that it is a good morning whether I want it or not; or that you feel good this morning; or that it is a morning to be good on?" "All of them at once," said Bilbo. (Tolkien 1973: 17–18)

Elsewhere I have explained the significance of this passage:

> Bilbo uses the token, "Good Morning!" to say several things "at once." He can do this because the sign that he uses bears multiple meanings. This token's bearing multiple meanings is why Gandalf replies, "What do you mean?" In response, we learn that Bilbo says different things by means of the same ambiguous token. Bilbo can say so many things because of the ambiguity of the sign and the different contexts (the sun is shining, the grass is green, Bilbo speaks to Gandalf, etc.) in which Bilbo uses it. Bilbo exploits the ambiguity of this sign to say many things "all [. . .] at once."

> What is perplexing is whether there are any limits to what Bilbo is saying. How vast is the range of things that can be said by means of an ambiguous sign? It is reasonable to suppose that the range is limited by whatever semantic or syntactic properties the sign bears and the contexts (indices) in which an ambiguous sign is used. [...]. For now I only wish to suggest that ambiguous signs are context-sensitive like indexicals.
>
> [...] In this (all too brief) summary of indexicals we see that the referent of an indexical expression like "I," and the proposition entailed by it, depends upon the person using the token of "I." Moreover, an indexical expression like "I" automatically refers to the person using it. Lastly, we see that *numerically the same* token of an expression can be relative to diverse contexts and so be used to affirm diverse propositions. (Williams 2013: 82)

According to this Conciliar Social model, there are mental sentence-tokens that bear semantic and syntactic attributes. Such mental sentence-tokens may include the essential indexical "I" and the copula. The reference of "I" is determined by an agent using it. The copula can be used to express different relations. Each divine hypostasis is an agent because each has causal powers and can exercise them. But, since the divine hypostases share *numerically the same* divine essence, nature, powers, acts of intellect, and acts of will, it follows that the divine hypostases share numerically the same use of numerically the same mental sentence-token. So, it is impossible for one and only one divine hypostasis to use a mental sentence-token and the other divine hypostases not share in numerically the same use of numerically the same mental sentence-token. Consequently, if God the Father uses a mental sentence-token "I am divine," and God the Father is aware of a proposition expressed by this sentence-token in the context of being used by God the Father, then the Father has *de se* knowledge, namely that <I am divine>. The copula here expresses the relation of numerical predication. Given the ontology, it is impossible for only God the Father to use this divine mental sentence-token. It is also true that God the Son and God the Holy Spirit share numerically the same use of numerically the same sentence token "I am divine." This means that the Son and Holy Spirit are aware of slightly different propositions, even though the Son and the Holy Spirit share numerically the same use of numerical the same mental sentence-token. For, God the Father is aware that they (sg.), God the Father, are divine; God the Son is aware that they (sg.), God the Son, are divine; and God the Holy Spirit is aware that they (sg.), God the Holy Spirit, are divine. Since there are three agents (Father, Son, and Holy Spirit), each one contributes to the reference of "I." In this case, the Father + use of "I" entails a reference to the Father; the Son + use of "I" entails reference to the Son; and the Holy Spirit + use of "I" entails reference to the Holy Spirit.

William Hasker has challenged this account (Hasker 2018; 2021a; 2021b) and I have responded (Williams 2020a; 2021). One of Hasker's objections has to do with the number of mental acts. For Hasker, a mental act just is an act directed at a proposition. He may be taken to suggest that a mental act is unstructured. But I propose that a mental act is structured. According to my account, through one shared mental act each divine hypostasis knows a different proposition. By my saying that there are three known propositions, Hasker infers that there must be three mental acts, and not one mental act. I respond by saying that a mental act is intrinsically structured; this internal structure explains why the act in question expresses the proposition that it expresses. In the case of all three divine hypostases sharing numerically the same use of numerically the same mental sentence-token of "I am divine," there are three overlapping structures in this use of "I am divine." The structure consists of (i) the use of the mental sentence-token, (ii) a *measure* relation, and (iii) a *measured by* relation. In the case of the essential indexical "I," the agent using it *measures* the use of "I." Since there are three divine agents sharing numerically the same use of "I," it follows that there are three *measures* of this use. Furthermore, this shared use of "I" is *measured by* God the Father, *measured by* God the Son, and *measured by* God the Holy Spirit. Here is my response to Hasker's question about the number of mental acts, beginning with the conditions for the divine hypostases's shared use of "I am divine":

Case 1: God the Father is *de se* aware of themself (sg.) being divine if and only if:
(1.i)  God the Father shares (with all other divine persons) numerically the same use of numerically the same divine mental token of "I am divine."
(1.ii)  God the Father *measures* the shared use of "I am divine."
(1.iii)  The shared use of "I am divine" is *measured by* God the Father.

Case 2: God the Son is *de se* aware of themself (sg.) being divine if and only if:
(2.i)  God the Son shares (with all other divine persons) numerically the same use of numerically the same divine mental token of "I am divine."
(2.ii)  God the Son measures the shared use of "I am divine."
(2.iii)  The shared use of "I am divine" is measured by God the Son.

Case 3: God the Holy Spirit is *de se* aware of themself (sg.) being divine if and only if:
(3.i)  God the Holy Spirit shares (with all other divine persons) numerically the same use of numerically the same divine mental token of "I am divine."
(3.ii)  God the Holy Spirit *measures* the shared use of "I am divine."
(3.iii)  The shared use of "I am divine" is *measured by* God the Holy Spirit.

How many mental acts are there? Well, it depends on what you mean by a "mental act." For many Social Trinitarians, their attention has been drawn to what's on the left-hand side of the "if and only if." If we focus on that, we'll be tempted (perhaps like Hasker) to posit that there's just one mental act for each proposition that is known. For, he says, "To be aware of a proposition is precisely to perform a mental act." But if we look at the right-hand side of the "if and only if," we get a complex ontological account because it is attentive to specific facts, such as the fact that the one who says "I" contributes to the meaning of "I." But what does this mean, ontologically speaking? In my analysis, this requires (i)–(iii) in each case.

So, how many "mental acts" are there? It depends on what we are talking about. If we focus only on what we might label the phenomenology, that is, the left-hand side of the "if and only if," then we might be tempted to say that there are three unshared "mental acts." (So: The Father's act of being self-aware, the Son's act of being self-aware, and the Holy Spirit's act of being self-aware.) And, if we suppose that, then we might be tempted to assert that there are (or must be) three distinct mental powers for each unshared mental act. So, we'd be led to counting the number of divine persons by the number of unshared "mental acts," understood as what's on the left-hand side of the "if and only if." That's how Hasker would seem to reason. And it is this way of reasoning that seems to lead him to disagree with the pronouncements of Constantinople III (at least, that is how one might reconstruct his reasoning). (Williams 2021: 532–533)

The Conciliar Social model also accounts for cases in which what is in the predicate position picks out something unique to one divine hypostasis. Consider whether the divine hypostases share numerically the same use of numerically the same sentence-token of "I am God the Son." God the Son could use this and be aware of a true proposition <I am God the Son>. The copula here expresses numerical identity. But, if the other divine hypostases share this use of this sentence-token, and the copula were to express numerical identity, then the Father and Holy Spirit would think (or believe) something that is false. (The Father is not numerically identical to the Son; and the Holy Spirit is not numerically identical to the Son.) But since all divine hypostases are omniscient, it follows that the copula does not express numerical identity but some other relation. Whatever this other relation is, it is not classical numerical identity. I suggest that the other relation expressed here is essential numerical sameness without (classical) identity. For, the relation here is between divine hypostases; the referent of "I" is one divine hypostasis and the referent of the predicate is a different divine hypostasis. Relative to God the Father, the proposition expressed by the use of the sentence-token ("I am God the Son") is <I am essentially numerically the same divine nature as, without being

identical to, the Son>. Similarly, relative to God the Holy Spirit, the proposition expressed is <I am essentially numerically the same divine nature as, without being identical to, the Son>. So, the divine hypostases share numerically the same use of a divine mental token, but each is aware of a different *de se* proposition. Just as the intension and extension of the indexical term "I" is relative to the divine hypostasis using it, so too is the relation expressed by the copula relative to the divine hypostasis using it.

## 6 Trinity and Simplicity

### 6.1 Conciliar Trinitarianism, Extensions, and Simplicity

Divine *simplicity* is one of the attributes ascribed by traditional theologians to the divine essence or nature. Typically, simplicity of the divine essence entails that there is no real composition. And real composition entails distinct things, entities, or what-have-you, which contingently compose something. However, as David Bradshaw has pointed out (2004: 234–242, 272–275), there is a significant disagreement between the Greek and Latin traditions regarding divine simplicity. The Greek side affirms the simplicity of the divine essence, and accepts contingency and numerical distinction between divine activities ("energeia") regarding creatures. By contrast, the Latin side accepts simplicity of the divine essence, but denies contingency and numerical distinction between divine activities regarding creatures, on the assumption that the divine essence is numerically identical to (or merely formally distinct from) divine activities regarding creatures (see Section 6.2 on formal distinction). However, this disagreement shows up between specific Greek and Latin theologians. It does not show up in Conciliar Trinitarianism as such.

According to Timothy Pawl, the first seven ecumenical councils do not explicitly teach divine simplicity (2016: 53). There is no text in the first seven ecumenical councils in which the word for simplicity is explained or defined. The closest comment regarding divine simplicity is indirect, in Pope Leo's *Tome*, which was endorsed by the council at Chalcedon in AD 451. Pope Leo wrote of "the God, whose will is indistinguishable from his goodness [...]." There are different ways that such a statement can be interpreted philosophically. (Is it the claim that God's will and goodness have the same intension, or the same extension, or both? Or is the claim that God's will is necessarily good such that it is impossible that God's will not be good?) If we are to be hermeneutically careful, any such interpretation might be hasty as an account of what divine simplicity would require. We just don't find any specification about divine simplicity in the first seven ecumenical councils.

If we look beyond these councils to later councils – what we might call Conciliar Extensions – there are statements that mention divine simplicity. But these do not provide a philosophical definition. For example, the Roman Catholic church has declared that the divine essence or nature is entirely simple (*simplex omnino*) (see Tanner 1990: 230, 232, 805). It is important to note that these statements are about the divine essence or nature; they do not apply to the divine hypostases as such. Lateran IV says, "We firmly believe and simply confess [. . .] three persons but one absolutely simple essence, substance or nature" (Tanner 1990: 230). This Roman Catholic council affirms that "simplicity" applies to the divine essence or nature that the divine hypostases share in common. It is not said that "simplicity" applies to the divine hypostases as such. At root, simplicity is a negative attribute of the divine essence or nature. Regarding the divine essence and nature, there is no real composition; there are no contingent parts, whether contingent physical parts or contingent metaphysical parts. (Some mainline Protestants and Reformed Orthodox also affirm divine simplicity, though there were competing explanations [see Muller 2003: 271–298].)

The Eastern Orthodox churches have not defined simplicity in a philosophically precise or fine-grained way. The Eastern Orthodox council of Blachernae in AD 1351 endorsed a statement of the faith by Gregory Palamas. In this statement, Gregory ascribes simplicity to the divine essence, nature, powers, and actions, but does not define simplicity (see Papadakis 1969: 389–342). Simplicity seems to imply that there cannot be but three divine hypostases (Father, Son, Holy Spirit), and that whatever it means, it is meant to be consistent with numerically different divine actions in the created world. It is plausible that simplicity does not require or imply numerical identity. If so, then this council would be inconsistent with Aquinas's account according to which the divine essence and divine actions are numerically identical (Bradshaw 2004: 242–250).

## 6.2 Thomas Aquinas's Problem Isn't a Conciliar Problem: Identity versus Nonidentity

As theologians have pointed out, there are different definitions or descriptions of divine simplicity (Radde-Gallwitz 2009; McCall 2012).

> To say that God is simple is to deny that there is any composition in God whatsoever. This implies that there are no material parts that come together to constitute God. But it also implies that the apparently diverse attributes people customarily ascribe to God are not diverse after all: or at least not diverse in the way that properties of objects of our ordinary experience are diverse. (Radde-Gallwitz 2009: 1–2)

A common claim about divine simplicity is that it entails that there is no real composition. There are different ways of specifying what the denial of real composition requires. Radde-Gallwitz describes two general theories, which he calls the "identity thesis" and the "propria thesis."

According to the "identity thesis," divine simplicity entails that all divine attributes are numerically identical to the one divine essence (see Brower 2008: 5–7). However, it doesn't follow from accepting this that one must also hold that numerical identity obtains between each divine hypostasis and the one divine essence. But Thomas Aquinas does suggest that each divine hypostasis is numerically identical to the one divine essence. For Aquinas, if we compare each divine hypostasis and the one divine essence, then there is no real (mind-independent) difference whatsoever between them. They are identically the same thing or being (see Friedman 2010: 13; Aquinas 1945: 285, which is *Summa Theologiae* Part 1, Question 28, Article 2), "in God relation and essence do not differ in being from each other but are one and the same"). But, if we compare, for example, the Father and the Son, then they are different from each other. The problem is that if the Father is numerically identical to the one divine essence, and the Son is numerically identical to the one divine essence, then (by transitivity of identity) it follows that the Father is numerically identical to the Son. But that consequence is false, and it contradicts Conciliar Trinitarianism.

Some interpreters of Aquinas argue that Aquinas denies transitivity here so as to avoid the unacceptable logical consequence (see Spencer 2017: 126). But, according to Christopher Hughes (1989: 187–240, esp. 230–239), this proposed weaker identity relation is at odds with Aquinas's texts overall, and with Aquinas's account of divine simplicity. What Hughes calls the weaker identity relation is what Jc Beall calls *subclassical* identity. If Spencer were right about Aquinas, then Aquinas would face the same problems that Beall's contradictory Trinitarianism faces (see Section 2.3). For on Aquinas's account of simplicity, there is no incommunicable (unshared) act or entity by which one divine hypostasis is not numerically identical to any other divine hypostasis, or to the one divine essence. If the Father is numerically identical to the divine essence, and the divine essence is numerically identical to the Son, then the Father is numerically identical to the Son. The fundamental problem with Aquinas's account is in saying that each divine hypostasis is numerically identical to the one divine essence. For Aquinas, there *is no* real ontological item that really distinguishes the divine hypostases. Moreover, this seems to contradict Conciliar Trinitarianism. If the ontology expressed by the claim that (i) the one divine essence just is the Father, Son, and Holy Spirit is equivalent to the ontology expressed by the claim that (ii) there is "one hypostasis of three names" (i.e., the divine essence is the Father, the Son, and the Holy Spirit) (see Section 2.2), then Aquinas's account contradicts Constantinople III.

One way to resolve Aquinas's fundamental problem is to deny that each divine hypostasis is numerically identical to the one divine essence, and to affirm that what distinguishes each divine hypostasis from the one divine essence is a real act or entity that is not the same real act or entity that is the one divine essence. But this affirmation would require Aquinas to give up his theory of real relations according to which a real relation is numerically identical to its absolute foundation (see Emery 2007: 94–96). This is precisely the route that Aquinas's critic Henry of Ghent took in his own Trinitarian theology (see Section 3.5; Williams 2012).

Some scholastic theologians after Thomas Aquinas challenged, in different ways, Aquinas's "identity thesis" regarding divine simplicity and the Trinity. For example, Henry of Ghent denies that divine simplicity requires only one being (*esse*) regarding the Trinity. He contends that there is the absolute (nonrelative) being (*esse*) of the divine essence, and a relative being (*esse ad aliud*) for each divine hypostasis. (Note for Aquinas that a real relation does not have its own *esse*; rather it is only an *ad aliud* [toward another], not an *esse ad aliud* [*being* toward another].) Each divine hypostasis consists of the one absolute being *and* a relative being. Consequently, no divine hypostasis is numerically identical to the one divine essence or being. Instead, for Henry, each divine hypostasis is necessarily numerically the same absolute "thing" or "being" as the one divine essence, but not identical to that one thing or being (see Williams 2012).

Likewise, Duns Scotus denies that a divine hypostasis is numerically identical to the one divine essence (1956: 260–274). Rather, a formal distinction obtains between them. A formal distinction is a kind of real distinction in that it is mind-independent, but the things in question are ontologically inseparable. Scotus gives different accounts of his formal distinction (see Cross 2004). One gloss expresses the distinction using a negation, that is, formal nonidentity. According to formal nonidentity, for example, divine goodness is *not* formally identical to divine wisdom, and vice versa. The other gloss expresses the distinction in a positive manner: Each divine attribute is a positive formality (a thing [*res*]). Hence, each divine attribute has its own definition or description, and the referent for each definition or description is a different formality (or thing). These formalities are really the same in the sense that they are ontologically inseparable from each other. Given this formal distinction, Duns Scotus maintains that although divine simplicity entails that there is no real composition (which requires ontological separability between different real things), no parts of any kind, no potentiality that is contrary to actuality, and no accidents (i.e., contingent properties that would actualize a potentiality), it does not follow that there is just one real divine attribute. Likewise, regarding the Trinity, each divine hypostasis is formally distinct from the one (trope of the) divine essence. There is not, so far as I can see, a logical problem for Henry of Ghent's or Duns Scotus's accounts of divine simplicity and the Trinity like there is for Thomas Aquinas's account.

Henry of Ghent and Duns Scotus are hardly the only theologians who reject the "identity thesis" account of divine simplicity and the Trinity. According to Andrew Radde-Gallwitz (2009: 177–208), Basil of Caesarea and Gregory of Nyssa claim that the divine attributes are irreducibly different *propria* (necessary attributes) of the divine essence. This is the "propria thesis." The divine names or titles like goodness, justice, and so on refer to attributes that are around the divine essence. These attributes are not numerically identical to the divine essence, but they are inseparable from it. Likewise, each divine hypostasis is not numerically identical to the one divine essence, for each consists of an unshareable "idioma" and the common divine essence (including the common attributes). In *Epistle 214*, Basil reports that even Latin-speaking Christians adopted the Greek term "ousia" to say that a divine hypostasis and the one divine nature are *not identical*: "The non-identity of hypostasis and ousia is [*hupostasis kai ousia ou tauton esti*], I take it, suggested even by our western brethren [. . .]" (1989: 254). They do not endorse numerical identity between the divine essence and the divine hypostases, but instead hold that they are inseparable.

Gregory of Nyssa appealed to divine simplicity to argue against Eunomius that there are not degrees of goodness between the divine hypostases, nor in the divine essence. Simplicity rules out a mixture of opposition between good and evil (nongood) in all divine hypostases (see Gregory of Nyssa 1986: 157; Radde-Gallwitz 2009: 177–218). The divine hypostases are simply good, with no possibility of a mixture with evil. (Though outside the scope of this Element, it is noteworthy that these Greek theologians are okay with the thought that simplicity is compatible with *contingent* divine energies [activities] in relation to creatures, including the energies of God in the life of a believer. Whatever the divine hypostases are and do, they are simply good, unmixed with any evil or opposition to the good, including their contingent divine energies. See Bradshaw 2004: 221–262.)

There is no logical problem with simplicity and the Trinity regarding Conciliar Trinitarianism. For, the first seven ecumenical councils do not make any precise claims about the Trinity and simplicity. There isn't enough propositional content even for there to be prima facie logical inconsistency. But there is a fundamental problem for those who posit the identity thesis interpretation of simplicity and apply it to the Trinity. For these theologians, including Thomas Aquinas, there is incoherence. But this is no problem for Conciliar Trinitarianism.

# References

Abramowski, Luise and Alan E. Goodman (1972). *A Nestorian Collection of Christological Texts*. Cambridge: Cambridge University Press.

Adamson, Peter (2020). Yahya Ibn 'Adi against Al-Kindi on the Trinity. *Journal of Eastern Christian Studies* 72.3–4: 241–271.

Anatoloios, Khaled (2011). *Retrieving Nicaea: The Development and Meaning of Trinitarian Doctrine*. Grand Rapids, MI: Baker Academic.

Aquinas, Thomas (1945). *Basic Writings of Saint Thomas Aquinas*. Anton Pegis, trans., New York: Random House.

(1975). *Summa Contra Gentiles IV: Salvation*. Charles J. O'neill, trans., South Bend, IN: University of Notre Dame Press.

Athanasius (2011). Letters to Serapion on the Holy Spirit. In *Works on the Spirit*. Mark DelCogliano, Andrew Radde-Gallwitz, and Lewis Ayres, eds. and trans., Yonkers, NY: St. Vladimir's Seminary Press: 53–137.

Ayres, Lewis (2004). *Nicaea and Its Legacy: An Approach to Fourth-Century Trinitarian Theology*. Oxford: Oxford University Press.

Barth, Karl (2004). *Church Dogmatics I.1: The Doctrine of the Word of God*. London: T&T Clark.

Basil the Great (1989). *The Treatise De Spiritu Sancto, the Nine Homilies of the Hexaemeron and the Letters of Saint Basil the Great*. Blomfield Jackson, trans., Edinburgh: T&T Clark.

(2011). *On the Holy Spirit*. Stephen Hildebrand, trans., Yonkers, NY: St. Vladimir's Seminary Press.

Batilo, Xavier (2018). La Distinction *gennetos/agennetos* dans le *Contra Eunomium I*. In *Gregory of Nyssa: Contra Eunomium I: An English Translation with Supporting Studies*, Miguel Brugarolas, ed., Leiden: Brill: 538–556.

Beall, Jc (2023). *Divine Contradiction*. Oxford: Oxford University Press.

Bradshaw, David (2004). *Aristotle East and West: Metaphysics and the Division of Christendom*. Cambridge: Cambridge University Press.

Branson, Beau (2022). One God, the Father: The Neglected Doctrine of the Monarchy of the Father, and Its Implications for the Analytic Debate about the Trinity. *Theologica* 6.2: 6–58.

Brower, Jeffrey (2004). The Trinity. In *The Cambridge Companion to Peter Abelard*. J. Brower and K. Guilfoy, eds., Cambridge: Cambridge University Press: 223–257.

(2008). Making Sense of Divine Simplicity. *Faith and Philosophy* 25.1: 3–30.

Brower, Jeffrey and Michael Rea (2005). Material Constitution and the Trinity. *Faith and Philosophy* 22: 57–76.

Cartwright, Richard (1987). *Philosophical Essays*. London: The MIT Press.

Coakley, Sarah (2002). What Does Chalcedon Solve and What Does It Not? Some Reflections on the Status and Meaning of the Chalcedonian "Definition". In *The Incarnation: An Interdisciplinary Symposium on the Incarnation of the Son of God*. Stephen T. Davis, Daniel Kendall SJ, and Gerald O'Collins SJ, eds., Oxford: Oxford University Press: 143–163.

Craig, William Lane (2005). Does the Problem of Material Constitution Illuminate the Doctrine of the Trinity? *Faith and Philosophy* 22.1: 77–86.

(2009). Toward a Tenable Social Trinitarianism. In *Philosophical and Theological Essays on the Trinity*. Thomas McCall and Michael Rea, eds., Oxford: Oxford University Press: 89–99.

Cross, Richard (2004). Scotus's Parisian Teaching on Divine Simplicity. In *Duns Scot a Paris: Actes du colloque de Paris, 2–4 septembre 2002*. Olivier Boulnois, Elizabeth Karger, Jean-Luc Solère, and Gérard Sondag, eds., Textes et Etudes du Moyen Age, 26. Leiden: Brepols: 519–562.

(2005). *Duns Scotus on God*. Burlington, VT: Ashgate.

DelCogliano, Mark (2010). *Basil of Caesarea's Anti-Eunomian Theory of Names: Christian Theology and Late-Antique Philosophy in the Fourth Century Trinitarian Controversy*. Leiden: Brill.

Denzinger, Henricus, ed. (1965). *Enchiridion Symbolorum: Definitionum et Declarationum De Rebus Fidei et Morum, Editio XXXIII*. Rome: Herder.

Didymus the Blind (2011). On the Holy Spirit. In *Works on the Spirit*. Mark DelCogliano, Andrew Radde-Gallwitz, and Lewis Ayres, eds. and trans., Yonkers, NY: St. Vladimir's Seminary Press: 143–227.

Duns Scotus, John (1956). *Ordinatio. Liber Primus. Distinctiones 4–10. Volume 4*. Carolo Balić, Martino Bodewig, Stanislao Buselic, et al., eds., Vatican: Typis Polyglottis Vaticanis.

Ebeid, Bishara (2021). Metaphysics of Trinity in Graeco-Syriac Miaphysitism: A Study and Analysis of the Trinitarian Florilegium in MS British Library Add. 14532. *Studia Graeco-Arabica* 11.1: 83–128.

Ebied, Rifaat Y., Albert Van Roey, and Lionel R. Wickham (1981). *Peter of Callinicum: Anti-Tritheist Dossier*. Leuven: Department Oriëntalistiek.

Emery, Giles OP (2007). *The Trinitarian Theology of Saint Thomas Aquinas*. Francesca Aran Murphy, trans., Oxford: Oxford University Press.

Erismann, Christopher (2010). Non Est Natura Sine Persona: The Issue of Uninstantiated Universals from Late Antiquity to the Early Middle Ages. In *Methods and Methodologies: Aristotelian Logic East and West: 500–1500*. Margaret Cameron and John Marenbon, eds., Leiden: Brill: 75–92.

Francisco de Vitoria (1991). *The Political Writings of Francisco de Vitoria.* Cambridge: Cambridge University Press.

Friedman, Russell L. (2007). The Voluntary Emanation of the Holy Spirit: Views of Natural Necessity and Voluntary Freedom at the Turn of the Thirteenth Century. In *Trinitarian Theology in the Medieval West.* Pekka Karkkainen, ed., Finland: Luther-Agricola-Society: 124–148.

(2010). *Medieval Trinitarian Thought from Aquinas to Ockham.* Cambridge: Cambridge University Press.

Gregory of Nazianzus (2002). *On God and Christ: The Five Theological Orations and Two Letters to Cledonius.* Frederick Williams and Lionel Wickham, trans., Yonkers, NY: St. Vladimir's Seminary Press.

(2003). *Select Orations.* Martha Vinson, trans., Washington, DC: Catholic University of America Press.

Gregory of Nyssa (1954). *The Lord's Prayer, the Beatitudes.* Hilda C. Graef, trans., New York: Paulist Press.

(1986). Concerning We Should Think of Saying that There Are Not Three Gods to *Ablabius.* In *The Trinitarian Controversy.* William G. Rusch, trans., Philadelphia, PA: Fortress Press: 149–161.

(2019). *Catechetical Discourse.* Yonkers, NY: St. Vladimir's Seminary Press.

Gregory Palamas (2022). *The Apodictic Treatises on the Procession of the Holy Spirit.* Tagarades: Uncut Mountain Press.

Grillmeier, Alois (1975a). "Piscatorie" – "Aristotelice". Zur Bedeutung der "Formel" in den seit Chalkedon getrennten Kirchen. In *Mit Ihm und in Ihm. Christologische Forschungen und Perspektiven.* Freiburg: Herder: 283–300.

(1975b). *Christ in Christian Tradition: Volume One: From the Apostolic Age to Chalcedon (451).* John Bowden, trans., Atlanta, GA: John Knox Press.

(1986). *Christ in Christian Tradition: Volume Two, Part One: From Chalcedon to Justinian I.* Pauline Allen and John Cawte, trans., Atlanta, GA: John Knox Press.

Grillmeier, Alois and Theresia Hainthaler (1995). *Christ in Christian Tradition: Volume 2, Part 2: The Church of Constantinople in the Sixth Century.* Pauline Allen and John Cawte, trans., Louisville, KY: John Knox Press.

(1996). *Christ in Christian Tradition: Volume 2, Part 4: The Church of Alexandria with Nubia and Ethiopia after 451.* O. C. Dean, trans., Louisville, KY: John Knox Press.

(2013). *Christ in Christian Tradition: Volume 2, Part 3: The Churches of Jerusalem and Antioch from 451 to 600.* Marianne Ehrhardt, trans., Oxford: Oxford University Press.

Harrison, Nonna Verna (2011). The Trinity and Feminism. In *The Oxford Handbook of the Trinity*. Gilles Emery, OP, and Matthew Levering, eds., Oxford: Oxford University Press.

Hasker, William (2013). *Metaphysics and the Tri-Personal God*. Oxford: Oxford University Press.

(2018). Can a Latin Trinity Be Social? Response to Scott M. Williams. *Faith and Philosophy* 35.3: 356–366.

(2021a). Is the Latin Social Trinity Defensible? A Rejoinder to Scott M. Williams. *Faith and Philosophy* 38.4: 505–513.

(2021b). "Latin" or "Conciliar", but Still Incoherent: A Rejoinder to Scott M. Williams. *Faith and Philosophy* 38.4: 540–545.

(2023). In Defense of the Trinitarian Processions. *Roczniki Filozoficzne* 71.2: 59–72.

Henry of Ghent (1953). *Henry of Ghent: Summae Quaestionum Ordinariarum (Reprint of the 1520 edition)*. St. Bonaventure, NY: The Franciscan Institute.

(2015). *Henry of Ghent's Summa, Articles 53–55: On the Divine Persons*. Roland J. Teske, SJ, trans., Milwaukee, WI: Marquette University Press.

(2021). *Henrici De Gandavo, Summa (Quaestiones ordinariae) art. LVI-LIX*. Gordon A. Wilson, Girard J. Etzkorn, Bernd Goehring, eds., Leuven: Leuven University Press.

Hill, Wesley (2015). *Paul and the Trinity: Persons, Relations, and the Pauline Letters*. Grand Rapids, MI: Eerdmans.

Holmes, Stephen R. (2012). Trinitarian Action and Inseparable Operations: Some Historical and Dogmatic Reflections. In *Advancing Trinitarian Theology: Explorations in Constructive Dogmatics*. Oliver Crisp and Fred Sanders, eds., Grand Rapids, MI: Zondervan: 60–74.

Hughes, Christopher (1989). *On a Complex Theory of a Simple God: An Investigation in Aquinas' Philosophical Theology*. Ithaca, NY: Cornell University Press.

Ibn Sina (2007). The Salvation, Metaphysics 2:1–5. In *Classical Arabic Philosophy*. Jon McGinnis and David C. Reisman, eds., Indianapolis, IN: Hackett: 211–214.

Jacobs, Jonathan (2015). The Ineffable, Inconceivable, and Incomprehensible God: Fundamentality and Apophatic Theology. *Oxford Studies of Philosophy of Religion* 6: 158–176.

Jamieson, R. B. and Tyler R. Wittman (2022). *Biblical Reasoning: Christological and Trinitarian Rules for Exegesis*. Grand Rapids, MI: Baker Academic.

Jedwab, Joseph and John A. Keller (2019). Paraphrase and the Trinity. *Faith and Philosophy* 36.2: 173–194.

John of Damascus (2022). *On the Orthodox Faith*. Norman Russell, trans., Yonkers, NY: St. Vladimir's Seminary Press.

Kelly, J. N. D. (1968). *Early Christian Doctrines*. London: Adam and Charles Black.

Koons, Robert and Timothy Pickavance (2015). *Metaphysics: The Fundamentals*. Oxford: Wiley-Blackwell.

Korta, Kepa and John Perry (2019). Pragmatics. In *Stanford Encyclopedia of Philosophy*. (Spring 2020 Edition), Edward N. Zalta (ed.), https://plato.stanford.edu/archives/spr2020/entries/pragmatics/.

Leftow, Brian (2004a). Anti Social Trinitarianism. In *The Trinity: An Interdisciplinary Symposium on the Trinity*. Stephen T. Davis, Daniel Kendall, SJ, and Gerald O'Collins, SJ, eds., Oxford: Oxford University Press: 203–249.

(2004b). A Latin Trinity. *Faith and Philosophy* 21.3: 304–333.

(2007). Modes without Modalism. In *Persons: Human and Divine*. Peter Van Inwagen and Dean Zimmerman, eds., Oxford: Oxford University Press: 357–375.

Lombardo, Nicholas E. (2022). The "Monarchy" of God the Father. *International Journal of Systematic Theology* 24.3: 324–351.

Lowe, Can and Gillian Shaftoe (Forthcoming). Henry of Ghent on the Relational Character of Causal Powers. *Journal of the History of Philosophy*.

Neuner, J., SJ., and J. Dupuis, SJ (1982). *The Christian Faith in the Doctrinal Documents of the Catholic Church: Revised Edition*. New York: Alba House.

Maspero, Giulio (2023a). *The Cappadocian Reshaping of Metaphysics: Relational Being*. Cambridge: Cambridge University Press.

(2023b). *Rethinking the Filioque with the Greek Fathers*. Grand Rapids, MI: Eerdmans.

McCall, Thomas (2010). *Which Trinity? Whose Monotheism? Philosophical and Systematic Theologians on the Metaphysics of Trinitarian Theology*. Grand Rapids, MI: Eerdmans.

(2012). Trinity Doctrine, Plain and Simple. In *Advancing Trinitarian Theology: Explorations in Constructive Dogmatics*. Oliver Crisp and Fred Sanders, eds., Grand Rapids, MI: Zondervan: 42–59.

Mosser, Carl (2009). Fully Social Trinitarianism. In *Philosophical and Theological Essays on the Trinity*. Thomas McCall and Michael Rea, eds., Oxford: Oxford University Press: 131–150.

Muller, Richard A. (2003). *Post-Reformation Reformed Dogmatics: The Rise and Development of Reformed Orthodoxy, ca. 1520 to ca. 1725 (4 vols.)*. Grand Rapids, MI: Baker Academic.

Mullins, R. T. (2023). The Trinitarian Processions. *Roczniki Filozoficzne* 71.2: 33–58.

Origen of Alexandria (1992). *Treatise on the Passover and Dialogue of Origen with Heraclides and His Fellow Bishops on the Father, the Son, and the Soul*. Robert J. Daly, SJ, trans., New York: Paulist Press.

Otto, J. C. T. (1881). *Corpus Apologetarum Christianorum Saeculi Secundi*. Vol. 5, 3rd edition, Jena: Mauke. http://stephanus.tlg.uci.edu/Iris/Cite? 0646:009:19150.

Paasch, J T. (2010). Arius and Athanasius on the Production of God's Son. *Faith and Philosophy* 27.4: 382–404.

(2012). *Divine Production in Late Medieval Trinitarian Theology: Henry of Ghent, Duns Scotus, and William Ockham*. Oxford: Oxford University Press.

Page, Meghan D. (2021). Detachment Issues: A Dilemma for Beall's Contradictory Christology. *Journal of Analytic Theology* 9: 201–204.

Papadakis, Aristeides (1969). Gregory Palamas at the Council of Blachernae. *Greek, Roman, and Byzantine Studies* 10.4: 333–342.

Pawl, Timothy (2016). *In Defense of Conciliar Christology: A Philosophical Essay*. Oxford: Oxford University Press.

Percival, Henry R. (1988). *The Seven Ecumenical Councils of the Undivided Church*. In *Nicene and Post-Nicene Fathers of the Christian Church, 2nd series, volume 14, The Seven Ecumenical Councils*. Henry Percival, ed. and trans., Edinburgh: T&T Clark: 1–671.

Perry, John (1993). What Are Indexicals? In *The Problem of the Essential Indexical and Other Essays*. Oxford: Oxford University Press: 33–52.

Philoponus, John (2017). *Fragments on the Trinity*. In *The Cambridge Edition of Early Christian Writings, Volume 1: God*. Andrew Radde-Gallwitz, ed., and Ellen Muehlberger, trans. Cambridge: Cambridge University Press: 359–370.

Pierce, Madison N. (2020). *Divine Discourse in the Epistle to the Hebrews: The Recontextualization of Spoken Quotations of Scripture*. Society for New Testament Studies Monograph Series 178. Cambridge: Cambridge University Press.

Platti, Emilio (1994). Yahya ibn 'Adi and His Refutation of Al-Warraq's Treatise on the Trinity in Relation to His Other Works. In *Christian and Arabic Apologetics During the Abbasid Period (750-1258)*. Samir Khalil Samir and Jorgen S. Nielson, eds., Leiden: E.J. Brill: 172–191.

Prestige, G. L. (1969). *GOD in Patristic Thought*. London: SPCK.

Pruss, Alexander R. (2009). Brower and Rea's Constitutional Account of the Trinity. In *Philosophical and Theological Essays on the Trinity*. Thomas McCall and Michael Rea, eds., Oxford: Oxford University Press: 314–325.

Radde-Gallwitz, Andrew (2009). *Basil of Caesarea, Gregory of Nyssa, and the Transformation of Divine Simplicity*. Oxford: Oxford University Press.

Riedinger, Rudolf, ed. (1990). *Concilium Universale Constantinopolitanum Tertium. Series Secunda, Volumen Secundum, pars prima*. Berlin: Walter de Gruyter.

(1992). *Concilium Universale Constantinopolitanum Tertium. Series Secunda, Volumen Secundum, pars secunda*. Berlin: Walter de Gruyter.

Robertson, J. N. W. B. ed. and trans. (1899). *The Acts and the Decrees of the Synod of Jerusalem*. London: Thomas Baker.

Severus of Antioch (2004). *Severus of Antioch (The Early Christian Fathers)*. Pauline Allen and C. T. R. Hayward, trans., London: Routledge.

Siecienski, Edward (2010). *The Filioque: History of a Doctrinal Controversy*. Oxford: Oxford University Press.

Sijuwade, Joshua (2021). Monarchical Trinitarianism: A Metaphysical Proposal. *TheoLogica* 5.2: 41–80.

(2022). Building the Monarchy of the Father. *Religious Studies* 58.2: 436–455.

Smith, Brandon, ed. (2023). *The Trinity in the Canon: A Biblical, Theological, Historical, and Practical Proposal*. Grand Rapids, MI: Baker Academic.

Spencer, Mark K. (2017). The Flexibility of Divine Simplicity: Aquinas, Scotus, and Palamas. *International Philosophical Quarterly* 57.2: 123–139.

Stead, Christopher (1977). *Divine Substance*. Oxford: Oxford University Press.

Swain, Scott R. (2023). John. In *The Trinity in the Canon: A Biblical, Theological, Historical, and Practical Proposal*. Brandon D. Smith, ed., Brentwood, TN: B&H Academic: 177–217.

Swinburne, Richard (1994). *The Christian God*. Oxford: Oxford University Press.

Tanner, Norman P., SJ, ed. (1990). *Decrees of the Ecumenical Councils, Volumes 1–2*. Washington, DC: Georgetown University Press.

Tolkien, J. R. R. (1973). *The Hobbit, or There and Back Again*. Revised. New York: Ballantine Books.

Tuggy, Dale (2021a). Trinity. In *The Stanford Encyclopedia of Philosophy* (Winter 2021 Edition), Edward N. Zalta (ed.), https://plato.stanford.edu/archives/win2021/entries/trinity/.

(2021b). Hasker's Tri-Personal God vs. New Testament Theology. *European Journal for Philosophy of Religion* 13.1: 153–177.

Twombly, Charles (2015). *Perichoresis and Personhood: God, Christ, and Salvation in John of Damascus*. Eugene, OR: Pickwick.

Van Dyke, Christina (2019). Medieval Mystics on Persons: What John Locke Didn't Tell You. In *Persons: A History*. Antonia Lolordo, ed., Oxford: Oxford University Press: 123–153.

Van Inwagen, Peter (2009). And Yet They Are Not Three Gods, But One God. In *Philosophical and Theological Essays on the Trinity*. Thomas McCall and Michael Rea, eds., Oxford: Oxford University Press: 216–248.

(2011). Relational vs. Constituent Ontologies. *Philosophical Perspectives, Metaphysics* 25: 389–405.

(2022). Richard Cartwright on Logic and the Trinity. *Theologica* 6.2: 112–136.

Van Roey, Albert and Pauline Allen, ed. and trans. (1994). *Monophysite Texts of the Sixth Century*, Orientalia Lovaniensia Analecta 56. Leuven: Peeters.

Vigorelli, Illaria (2018). The *skesis* of the Father and of the Son in the *Contra Eunomium I*. In *Gregory of Nyssa: Contra Eunomium I: An English Translation with Supporting Studies*, Miguel Brugarolas, ed., Leiden: Brill: 538–556.

Wierenga, Edward (2004). Trinity and Polytheism. *Faith and Philosophy* 21.3: 281–294.

Williams, Scott M. (2010). Augustine, Thomas Aquinas, Henry of Ghent, and John Duns Scotus: On the Theology of the Father's Intellectual Generation of the Word. *Recherches de Théologie et Philosophie médiévales* 77.1: 38–81.

(2012). Henry of Ghent on Real Relations and the Trinity: The Case for Numerical Sameness without Identity. *Recherches de Théologie et Philosophie médiévales* 79.1: 109–148.

(2013). Indexicals and the Trinity: Two Non-social Models. *Journal of Analytic Theology* 1: 74–94.

(2017). Unity of Action in a Latin Social Model of the Trinity. *Faith and Philosophy* 34.2: 321–346.

(2019). Persons in Patristic and Medieval Christian Theology. In *Persons: A History*. Antonia Lolordo, ed., Oxford: Oxford University Press: 52–84.

(2020a). In Defense of a Latin Social Trinity: A Response to William Hasker. *Faith and Philosophy* 37.1: 96–117.

(2020b). Personhood, Ethics, and Disability: A Comparison of Byzantine, Boethian, and Modern Concepts of Personhood. In *Disability in Medieval Christian Philosophy and Theology*. Scott M. Williams, ed., Oxford: Routledge: 80–108.

(2021). Gregory of Nyssa, Conciliar Trinitarianism, and the Latin (or Conciliar) Social Trinity: Response to William Hasker. *Faith and Philosophy* 38.4: 514–539.

(2022a). Discovery of the Sixth Ecumenical Council's Trinitarian Theology: Historical, Ecclesial, and Theological Implications. *Journal of Analytic Theology* 10: 332–362.

(2022b). Why There Wasn't, and How There Can Be, a Latin Social Trinity. In *Claiming God: Essays in Honor of Marilyn McCord Adams*. Christine Helmer and Shannon Craigo-Snell, eds., Eugene, OR: Pickwick: 153–174.

(Forthcoming-a). *The Trinitarian Theology of Henry of Ghent*. TBD.

(Forthcoming-b). *Unity of Essence, But Trinity of Persons: Conciliar Trinitarianism and Analytic Theology*. Joshua Cockayne, Christa McKirland, and Jonathan Rutledge, eds., Eugene, OR: Cascade Books.

Zachhuber, Johannes (2020). *The Rise of Christian Theology and the End of Ancient Metaphysics: Patristic Philosophy from the Cappadocian Fathers to John of Damascus*. Oxford: Oxford University Press.

# Acknowledgments

While dedications are not allowed in Cambridge Elements, I acknowledge that in another possible world I am dedicating this Element to my parents Wilburn and Jacqueline Williams, and grandparents Kermit and Lois Williams. Thanks to Beau Branson for the many conversations about the Trinity and Greek theologians. Thanks to the two anonymous reviewers for helpful comments. Thanks to my department chair, Melissa Burchard, for supporting me in response to certain administrative obstacles. Lastly, thanks to my wife Lisa Toland Williams for her love and encouragement, for gardening together, and for garden walks with our double-dapple dachshunds, Origen and Didymus (who is blind), whose namesakes played significant roles in the history of Trinitarian theology.

.

## Cambridge Elements ≡

# The Problems of God

## Series Editor

### Michael L. Peterson

*Asbury Theological Seminary*

Michael L. Peterson is Professor of Philosophy at Asbury Theological Seminary. He is the author of *God and Evil* (Routledge); *Monotheism, Suffering, and Evil* (Cambridge University Press); *With All Your Mind* (University of Notre Dame Press); *C. S. Lewis and the Christian Worldview* (Oxford University Press); *Evil and the Christian God* (Baker Book House); and *Philosophy of Education: Issues and Options* (Intervarsity Press). He is co-author of *Reason and Religious Belief* (Oxford University Press); *Science, Evolution, and Religion: A Debate about Atheism and Theism* (Oxford University Press); and *Biology, Religion, and Philosophy* (Cambridge University Press). He is editor of *The Problem of Evil: Selected Readings* (University of Notre Dame Press). He is co-editor of *Philosophy of Religion: Selected Readings* (Oxford University Press) and *Contemporary Debates in Philosophy of Religion* (Wiley-Blackwell). He served as General Editor of the Blackwell monograph series Exploring Philosophy of Religion and is founding Managing Editor of the journal *Faith and Philosophy*.

## About the Series

This series explores problems related to God, such as the human quest for God or gods, contemplation of God, and critique and rejection of God. Concise, authoritative volumes in this series will reflect the methods of a variety of disciplines, including philosophy of religion, theology, religious studies, and sociology.

**Cambridge Elements** ⁼

# The Problems of God

## Elements in the Series

A full series listing is available at: www.cambridge.org/EPOG

Printed in the United States
by Baker & Taylor Publisher Services